The REASON WE ARE HERE

Make Our Powers Together to Realize God's Justice
—China Issue, Global Warming, and LGBT—

INCLUDING SPIRITUAL MESSAGES FROM GOD THOTH

RYUHO OKAWA

HS PRESS

Contents

2

Q&A Session

3

Master Okawa's Answers
To Canadian Activists

4

Spiritual Messages from God Thoth:
God of North America speaks His mind

Preface

The main content of this book is the English lecture that I gave on October 6, 2019 (Canada time), to commemorate the 33rd anniversary of Happy Science and my giving of over 3,000 lectures.

It also includes the answers to three questions from the Q&A session given on the day of the lecture, as well as my replies to the questions that I gave after returning to Japan from two activists who are working for the freedom of Hong Kong and an activist who is working for the freedom of Uyghur who are all living in Canada.

My answers are related to Canada, so I could not speak enough, but I tried to talk about what is "world justice".

In Japan, after six months since my lecture in Japan, the Asahi newspaper, who originally supported mainland China, clearly criticized the Hong Kong police's excessive brutality in their November editorial. It showed that Asahi newspaper supports the people of Hong Kong and the students who are demonstrating. The Japanese administration is not taking a clear stance, whether that's because they're thinking about President Xi Jinping's visit to Japan and hosting the Tokyo Olympics next year. The opposition parties are also avoiding this Hong Kong issue.

All of the answers and keys are in this book.

This is a fight between the atheistic, materialistic country and the faithful people of Hong Kong and Uyghur.

My thinking is to lead the Hong Kong Revolution to a bloodless revolution in mainland China. Even for the 1.4 billion people of China, it's a way to happiness for them to acquire faith, fundamental human rights, democracy, and freedom. And, it's also the royal road to prosperity.

I don't want Japan to be a country that easily accepts the law of the jungle and thinks about economic profit only. I pray that Japan becomes a country of over five percent economic growth and a God-believing country again, and acquires the power to change the worst totalitarian dictatorship since Hitler into a peaceful and democratic one. And, I want to realize the day in which the people of Hong Kong, Uyghur, Tibet, Inner Mongolia, and others are freed from fear. I strongly hope so.

Ryuho Okawa
Master & CEO of Happy Science Group
Nov. 15, 2019

1

The Reason We Are Here

Lecture given on October 6, 2019
The Westin Harbour Castle, Toronto, Canada

1

My Impression of Toronto

Hi. Hello, Toronto. Nice to meet you. Thank you. Thank you. Thank you very much.

OK. Yeah, this is my first lecture in Canada. A few days ago, I got through the airport gate, and one of the agents asked me, "Why are you here? Please teach me your purpose of journey." I answered, "I have one lecture in Toronto." She asked me, "What lecture is that?" I answered, "The theme is, 'The Reason We Are Here'." [*Audience laughs.*] She cannot understand my purpose, so I said, "Ah, except in Canada, I'm very famous." I said so. This is a reason we are here.

Yeah, it's the first time for me, "Who is Ryuho Okawa?" she asked. Even in India, with more than one billion population, they know about me. "Oh, I saw you on TV or poster or like that." Or, even in Hong Kong, the lady at the bookstore knew about me, and I asked her, "Would you take a photo with me?" and she hesitated. "No. In Hong Kong, it's not permitted," she said.

OK, OK. This is Canada, so I want to start a new type of lecture. I stayed for two or three days already, and the impression of Canada is very gentle, tender, and kind. And I've never met a really bad person in this country because of few population, maybe. But the country is very huge and your resources are very fertile, and you may have a big dream, "you can."

2

Canada is in Its Term of Election For the Next Prime Minister

And this is the term of election for next prime minister, so you are very busy in reality. I was asked about that. "Mr. Trudeau or Mr. Scheer, which do you like?" I cannot answer exactly. Both are good. Both are good leaders for Canada. But I just feel that, Mr. Trudeau said in his book, I mean *Common Ground*, "In Canada, Trudeau means responsibility." He said in that book. Trudeau is a famous name in Canada, and it's 'responsibility'. How about, then, Mr. Scheer? He said nothing about that, but he wants to get some responsibility about Canada.

We are not so huge in members in Canada, so I won't speak too much regarding next elections, but to tell the truth, I think Prime Minister Trudeau is like what we think, "This is Canadian-like thinking," he dispatches such kind of thinking. He is very gentle, and he is very kind and tolerant, and he is liberal-oriented. The final one... [*Smiling, he stops the audience from clapping*] No, stop. [*Audience laughs.*] The conclusion is quite different, so never praise about that.

But the final one, "liberal" is a deep word in that meaning. And in a common sense, to be liberal is not so bad. For example, if you use the word "liberal" in the totalitarian regime, you can destroy that type of country by the word "tolerant" or "liberal" or "democracy" or "freedom of speech" or "freedom of expression" or "freedom of political actions."

3

Canada Should Decide Pivotal Things

Too much liberalism leads to
The weakness of the country

You already can guess what I want to say. Yeah, I've heard that recently in Toronto, there was a collision regarding demonstration for Hong Kong problem. In Canada's opinion, if Canadian people are living in Hong Kong, they will support Hong Kong people, I guess so, because Canadian people maybe think that the gigantic Beijing China is a very totalitarian regime, and they easily deprive the freedom of the people. I think so. But I've heard that the demonstration made a great confusion because of the students from mainland China, and it's very famous worldwide, but I think the students from China have patriotism for their nation. I can understand about that.

But the Canadian people want to teach them that, "We are not the United States of America, but we are living next door to the United States of America, so we have almost the same tendency." Only to think too much tolerance and too much liberalism easily leads to weakness of this country. Canada doesn't have such kind of strongness of the United States, but the weakness, or just easily wants to be followers of strong countries. This is a problem of Canada. I guess so.

It's also the problem of Japan. I am the Founder and CEO of Happy Science Group, and we have a political party. Its name is Happiness Realization Party, in Japan. Only Happiness Realization Party made a demonstration in Japan for freedom of Hong Kong. Almost all Japanese people are just watching because they can understand the tragedy of Hong Kong people, but they cannot be tolerant about the declining of income from mainland China, so they keep silence. Japanese government also, or other political parties also, and common people also, mass media also. That is the situation of Japan.

Even Canada sent a battleship
Near Hong Kong

Japan cannot live by their country only. Here, in Canada, you have more than 150 percent food supply and you have a lot of resources, so in some meaning, you are very strong to survive. But Japan is not so good at the capability of how to survive in the near future, so they cannot decide on pivotal things.

Even in Canada, Prime Minister Trudeau cannot decide on a lot, especially pivotal things, I mean, very difficult but important things which are problems all over the world. For example, Hong

Kong problem. He sent one ship, battleship-type of ship, to the sea near Hong Kong. I've read, in Japan, about that. It's a good but curious decision. Even Trudeau sent military force. Oh, it's astonishing for Japanese people. He changed. Before the election, he changed a little.

4

What I Want to Say About Global Warming

Global warming has been the trend For the last 10,000 years

And another problem is, as you know, 16-year-old young lady, Ms. Greta Thunberg came to Canada and had a conversation with Mr. Trudeau for 15 minutes, and after that, Greta said, "Ah, you are going to do nothing!" He was scolded. He usually says, "I'm sorry." It's a Japanese way of thinking. So, yeah, indeed he's a good man, but he is indecisive. I think so. He's a prime minister. He doesn't have any need to talk with Ms. Greta Thunberg. She said global warming is the death of this modern society, and she scolded a lot of adults all over the world.

But I want to say that, she finally usually says, "It's a science. Obey science. Science is everything," like that. But I am older than her, so I've learned a lot. And now, I'm a spiritual master, so I know this 10,000 years' history of the people. I must say that Ice Age ended about 10,000 years ago, and then global warming has been keeping its trend and this Earth became warmer and warmer. It led to a lot of civilizations to flourish. She usually says that the emission of CO_2 is bad and carbon dioxide is harmful to humankind, but in the standpoint of science, it's not true.

Carbon dioxide—it means the plants of the Earth can absorb a lot of energy from the air and there can spread a lot of green in this world. It will feed animals in this world, and after that, a lot of people can live on this Earth. So, this has been the trend. Science can decide almost nothing about this one. And, I think the next age will be the beginning of the Ice Age, I mean the Glacial Age. So, you don't think too much about that.

Behind global warming theory lies Communist thinking

This kind of opinion is environment-friendly and it is common in the Canadian people, I think, but this opinion just attacks President Donald Trump's policy. I think so. And behind this opinion, there is some kind of communist thinking. Indeed, there is a lot of activity. So, we can't think so simply about that.

So, I want to say to you that you can prosper more and have industrialization and more population. It's not so bad. It's already considered in heaven. So, my opinion is not so major in the world, but please just think about that. It's not the science only. It's the limited science.

5

Real Responsibility Means World Justice

We must stop the poverty and war In the world

We just think about the more important thing. That is, for example, the poverty, how to solve the poverty of the world. Billions of people are suffering from poverty. How can we solve this problem? Please think about that. It's very important, and it's the mission of an advanced country, I think. Canada has the capacity to help the people of the poverty country, so you can produce more wealth to help them. I just want to say that, if "Trudeau" means "responsibility," its responsibility must be real responsibility to save the people of the world.

One is, stop the poverty of the world; another one is, stop the confusion or war of the world. We must engage in such kind of activities. You can, of course. Of course, Japan should do like that. We have potential, but both countries haven't done enoughly.

Deciding nothing means no responsibilities, Not tolerance

So, we must define the meaning of responsibility again. It's not "the peaceful way of living of your own nation" only. Responsibility means the world justice and what is the Truth of this Earth. I think so.

People of both sides will appear if you decide something. We know about that. But if you hesitate to decide, it only means not tolerance, but just floating over the global world. So you, Canadian people, must be one of the leaders of the world. You have such kind of power inside. Only a strong opinion is required. If you don't want to have any trouble and want to escape from any trouble, you can decide almost nothing, and it means no responsibilities. I think so.

6

The Common Base of Prosperity of Taiwan and Hong Kong

China has not experienced real democracy

I made a lecture in Taiwan also, this March, and at that place, I said, "The prosperity of Taiwan is based on their freedom and it's precious to keep their peace and their prosperity and the happiness of the people. No one can destroy the situation." And I sometimes say to Xi Jinping that, "China has not experienced real democracy in its 5,000 years." They cannot understand what I want to say.

Xi Jinping's guardian spirit, in my books, usually says that he cannot understand the meaning of democracy and the meaning of freedom of politics, voting or like that. It just means confusion. In China, historically, they required one-China policy. They are seeking for one China, and the total country, they wanted. They've not experienced real democracy, but in Hong Kong, there is.

The starting point of Umbrella Revolution And Hong Kong Revolution

I also made a lecture in Hong Kong in 2011. On the day of typhoon, there were more than 1,300 people there, and I asked them. They were thinking just to change their Hong Kong-like thinking to mainland China-like thinking, or escape from Hong Kong. They were thinking these two only. I indicated them, "There is a third way for you. Please change China through the prosperity of Hong Kong." This prosperity comes, one is from the faith to God, and one is from the freedom of the people— freedom of activity, freedom of thinking, freedom of expression, freedom of voting, and freedom of election, of course. These are the common base of prosperity.

I said to them, "So, Hong Kong people, you should be the teacher of next-age China. This is the third way." This was the first point for them, and three years later, there occurred the Umbrella Revolution in 2014. They were defeated at that time, but again, they made a demonstration, and now, I call it Hong Kong Revolution again.

7

China's Ethnic Suppression and Totalitarian Regime

Democracy and freedom
Will make China greater than as it is

I hope... Canada is between two powers, one is the democratic power, and another is the economic profit. China is intruding, but I dare say, I don't hate Chinese people. I like them. I love them. I want them to be happier. So, I ask them, "Why don't you experience democracy, or the freedom of speech or expression or voting?" It's one examination for them, but it will make them greater than as it is. It means they can be on the same ground to discuss with Western people. So, I ask them to do so.

This is the China problem, and China problem includes the Uyghur problem, and of course, Tibet problem and Inner Mongolia problem. They are suppressed a lot, but they are not broadcasted. This is a totalitarian regime. I already said it in Taiwan, the meaning of totalitarian regime. There are three symbols. One is, there is a mass murder, or violence on many people. And the second is the existence of secret police. And the third is the concentration camp. These three are the characteristics of totalitarian system. It was shown by Adolf Hitler in Germany, and also, it was shown by Stalin in Soviet Russia.

Checkpoint:
Belief in God and fundamental rights

"Communism and capitalism" is not the real dividing indication. But just think about two things: one is, "Is there any belief in God or not?" another one is, "Is there any fundamental rights in there or not?" This is very, very important. I love Chinese people, but in this regime, formally, Xi

Jinping denies the faith or the importance of faith. And also, they don't believe in communism. They are really using capitalism, especially in south part of China. They are just using communism by the Machiavellism-like meaning.

8

God is Not Dead

So, it's time to change, I think. World is required to change. More than one billion people are under the control of one policy or one person; this is apt to collapse the freedom and prosperity and faith of this Earth.

So, please teach the good things from Canada to such kind of countries. I think so. Especially, this country is, more than 75 percent are Christian, I've heard so. But in reality, there is no God in Canada because you have short history, so no one can consider more than 500 years ago. Just, you can imagine, "Two thousand years ago, there used to be Jesus Christ, but it's very far away from here. We don't know. Who is God, we don't know." This is a reality.

So, I want to say that

God is alive.
God is not dead.
God is watching you.
God is leading you.
God wants to save you,
Save such people who are suffering in this world
By dint of evil spirits or evil thinking
Or devil-like thinking.

God is fighting.
God has been fighting, even now.
So, please remake your religion
into a stronger one.
It is your responsibility, I think.

9

After Visiting the Gay Town In Toronto

A lost spirit appeared in my hotel room

And I have another idea regarding you. I visited the gay town, it's famous, especially in Toronto. And in this meaning, you are the leading country of the world. It is the appearance of tolerance or diversity or belief in the variety of the possibility.

But... I've been to gay town and saw the statue of Alexander Wood*, and I took a picture with the statue, but after that, I went back to the hotel and there appeared Alexander Wood. And he said to me, "I am the God. I am the new God of the future." But I asked him, "Where are you now?" He said he

---

* Alexander Wood (1772 - 1844) was the pioneer of the Gay Village in Toronto, Canada where homosexual people gather. The author had recorded "Spiritual Interview with Alexander Wood" on October 3 (Canada time), just three days before this lecture.

is living in gay town now. This means he cannot understand the real aspect of another world, where is heaven and where is hell. He cannot understand. But he thinks that he is the God of new age.

LGBT matter
In Christian and Japanese societies

So, this is just the pointing out of the problem. If you want to know a lot regarding this matter, please come to our branch office. I have a lecture already recorded. But now, I don't want to say anymore about this problem. This is a Canadian problem, but it's more than that; it's the Christian society's problem.

Japan is not a Christian society, but Japan is also aiming to change our constitution. Our Japanese constitution says that both male and female can marry, so Japan is just thinking about the amendment of constitution, but it's very difficult now, so they made laws only. Some cities set up that kind of law and people can make same-sex marriage in several cities in Japan, but it's not the total tendency.

10

The Reason We Are Here

The human soul is made of a group of souls

But I want to say, this is "the reason we are here." We are not a material being, a material existence only. God created human souls. It was a very ancient age. And after that, some space people, outer space people, joined in our earthly living. It's written in *The Laws of the Sun* [see Figure 1], as you have seen before this lecture. It's very difficult and confusing,

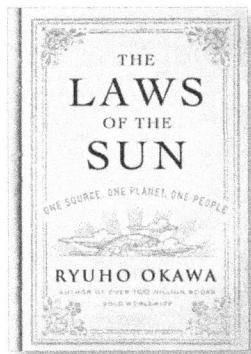

Figure 1.
The Laws of the Sun (New York: IRH Press, 2018)

but we have more than hundreds of millions of years' experience in this Earth living as a human being.

So, this is a weak point of Christianity. I must say that we, human beings, have souls before we are born into this world. We have past lives. Christians sometimes say that it's an evil thinking, but it's true. I examined more than 900 times and published more than 500 books about that. We have past lives. And one of them... I mean, we are a group. You heard that, "soulmate" or "soul brothers"-like words already. Yes, indeed. We have not one energy in us. We have several souls in our own group. One of them is born into this world, into this body, and grows up and goes back to heaven. This is the real explanation.

The human soul can be born As male or female

So, at first, God created both male and female, but our teachings show that the human soul can be born as male or female. Both are choiceable. You can choose both sides. When you are born as a man or when you are born as a woman, it means, during your lifetime in this world, several decades, you can acquire new character. And your new character, I mean, what you are, can be kept to the next reincarnation. This is the reality of spiritual aspect.

11

In This Materialistic World, Be Spiritual

So, we came here to experience a new age, a modern society, and make new character and go back to another world. Some become new angels through the education of this three-dimensional world, and some make mistakes and go down to hell. But it is also an experience. Hell is a hospital for them. They don't know clearly about their spirituality in their lives, so they are going to a hospital in the spiritual world. And after they awaken, they can go back to heaven.

So, all is teaching us
That the most important thing
Is to learn how to live in this world,
In your materialistic body.

But how you can realize
What you are and what you should do
Will decide your afterlife.
It's God's rule.
God does not divide or sentence you.
You, yourself, decide your destiny.

This is the reason
We are living in this world,
In Canada, in the United States,
Brazil, or Uganda, or other country
Who are watching my lecture now.

This is the reason. This world is materialistic, but in this materialistic world, be spiritual. That's the main reason of this life. Thank you very much.

2

Q&A Session

Lecture given on October 6, 2019
The Westin Harbour Castle, Toronto, Canada

1

New Faith to Spread
In North America

Q1

I would appreciate your advice about building Toronto Shoshinkan. Please come back to Canada again.

Canada has a lot of hidden power

RYUHO OKAWA

If I'll come to Canada next time, I want to use, instead of Air Canada, JAL or ANA, or like that. It's not so comfortable. I couldn't sleep even a minute. It might be the second time for me, even one minute I couldn't sleep. So, it means, not so many businessmen or important people come to Canada, and only sightseeing people come to Canada. I think so.

Indeed, Japanese people should know a lot about Canada, be more concerned about Canada. If we took survey in Japan, "Who is the prime minister of Canada?" less than 50 percent can answer that question. But Canada has a lot of capacity, I think, and Canada has a lot of hidden *daikokutens*. I think so. They are supporters for Happy Science.

Japanese people usually think "foreigner" means the people of the United States, but it's not enough, of course. Please teach what Canadians think about, and do something characteristic to other countries. You can do more than that.

Indeed, we need more members in Canada. This is another answer to, "The Reason We Are Here." "To become members of Happy Science," another answer is this one. Or, the reason we are here, "Because we want to be daikokutens."

Happy Science accepts
Believers of other religions

We are very tolerant. We are accepting people who are believers in other religions, for example, Islamic people or Christian people, Buddhist people or Japanese Shinto people. There are a lot of members who have such kind of belief in them because we are combined, and the founders of those religions were—at that time, almost all of the worldwide religions were taught by me from the heavenly world, so I know a lot about them. They are not different. We are seeking for the same direction, just save people and just want to make people happier. This is the "common ground" for us. So, believe in Happy Science.

In Japan, we have a lot of followers, for example, other political parties' members or other religious members. For example, in Japan, there's Jodo Shinshu, Shinran's teaching's followers. It has

10 million members, they say, but its top is our member. So, we have a lot of members outside of Happy Science, for example. And in India, we have a lot of members. We don't have enough branches, of course.

So, next stage is how to manage worldwide activities through breeding the leaders, and of course, thinking about the business mind-like thinking. Each leader must have such kind of thinking. I, myself, was, during my younger age, my twenties, a member of a trading house, and I worked on Wall Street. I can imagine a lot of branches all over the world, and can manage them. So, I know, and I have dreams of such kind.

Please ask our lecturers to attract a lot of people, more than as it is. If I go to Africa, there come more than tens of thousands of people. When I went to Uganda, there came three broadcasting companies including one national company. They broadcast my lecture, and more than 30 million people watched it. In Nepal, also the same; in India, also the same; and in Sri Lanka, also the same. It is a Buddhist country, so they came to see me.

God Thoth governs North America

But in Christian society, Western society, people already belong to churches, so they don't want to come on Sunday. But please teach them: I am a teacher of Jesus Christ. This was true, and this is true, now. So, please tell them. This is El Cantare, the meaning of El Cantare, meaning of Elohim, Allah, or ancient age God.

And, in this area, north part of the American continent, you have God. Its name is Thoth. Yeah, you have. Thoth is one of the soul brothers of El Cantare. He is the Almighty God of Atlantis age. He is. He is governing the spiritual world of Canada and the United States. So, you can believe in God. He is, and He is connected to me.

So, it's a new faith, but please spread these teachings. We need more members, I ask you. I want to save people who are suffering now. So, we need a lot of members and we need a lot of people who are influenced by our teachings, of course.

I will do my best. We have millions of followers all over the world outside of Japan, but main point is, the people of the world are not so wealthy. Some people have less than one percent of the income of the Japanese people. This is the difficulty of activities. So, please cooperate. I will think with you.

2

Helping Patients Who Suffer from Drug Abuse

Q2

I'm working at a hospital, as a registered nurse in Los Angeles, right now. I have so many people suffering from drug abuse, and I think this is a big problem in the United States and, I believe, in Canada too. Many people, like young age, 20 or 30 years old, they are not compliant, they don't care about their life. And we try to teach the truth of the soul, but their cap is like a big rock, so they don't understand what we are saying.

So, I just want to know how to help them, how to give them the Truth. Yeah, so that's my main concern. Every time, when I take care of the patient, they don't listen to us, nothing. They come back and forth, to and from the hospital, because they want to do drugs. Many people are suffering, and the country is losing much power because of that, because of the young-aged people all involved. So, I just want to know how to cope with this problem, in this country, and also in Japan too.

Pray for the power from heaven

RYUHO OKAWA

OK. Every country has its problem. Younger people have also problems and disease in heart. Yeah, it's very difficult to teach one by one because they acquired a lot of teachings for her or for him, or at his age or at her age, and thinking of parents has very much influence on them.

So, please meditate and pray for our heavenly guiding spirits. "Give me power to teach them. Give me power to persuade them. Give me power to save them." They will 100 percent assist you.

There comes light of the stream, and it will give you super power, supernatural power to save people. Your words are not your words. They come from heavenly existence, through your throat, through your mouth. You can teach them. At that time, at that situation, at the individual, for what he needs, you can speak to a T. You can, yes.

Just pray for the souls of angels or bodhisattva, nyorai of Happy Science. There are more than 500 great angels and angels in heaven, for our group. So, you can. You can receive their power, spiritual power, and you can do everything through them. Even the bad-thinking people can change into good-thinking people. Or, even people who are suffering from going more than point of no return, I mean, who are destined to die, you can call them back to this world and give them new lives.

Our next movie describes about that. So, please ask other people to watch *Immortal Hero*[*]. In it, I answer a lot regarding your question. So, my answer is, "Require the power from heaven." You can be stronger. That's the conclusion.

---

* The movie, Immortal Hero (executive producer and original story by Ryuho Okawa, released simultaneously on October 18, 2019 in Japan, the U.S., and Canada).

3

The Real Meaning of Golden Age

Q3

My question to you today is regarding the Golden Age that you spoke of in your book, *The Laws of the Sun*. You said that the Golden Age will be dawning in the year of 2020. I would like to know more in depth, what is the Golden Age, and what mindset must the countries of the world have to make sure the Golden Age is the most powerful success.

RYUHO OKAWA

OK. The real meaning of the Golden Age. It will begin from 2020, I already said. It means, we will destroy atheists or non-believers in God on this Earth, and such kind of great power will be ruined from 2020 to 2030. For example, it means the gigantic country who doesn't believe in God and is just one-party system and communism-only country, will be destroyed by dint of God's power [*audience applauds*].

And, another answer is, there are people who are living miserably in this world, for example, poverty, and another one is under the war situation. They cannot live actively and happily. We will stop such kind of situation and make peace in this world. It's Buddha Land Utopia. It's a meaning of Golden Age. OK?

And, *you* are the expected person, one of expected people for that. So, I will do my best, but it's not my limit or our limit. We have a lot of members who have hidden powers within them. So, we make our powers together! Together our power, do great things on this Earth! Is it OK? [*Audience applauds.*]

OK. Thank you. See you again.

3

Master Okawa's Answers
to Canadian Activists

Lecture given on October 11, 2019
Happy Science General Headquarters, Tokyo

This chapter is the transcript of the session recorded on October 11, 2019 at Happy Science General Headquarters. In the first part of the session, a video footage was shown; it was an on-site interview with three Canadian activists who attended the author's lecture, "The Reason We Are Here" on October 6 in Toronto, Canada. Then, two interviewers offered more detailed information on them, and the author gave his reply to each activist.

Activists

Gloria Fung,
Canada-Hong Kong Link, President

Sheng Xue,
Vice President, The Federation for a Democratic China
Vice President of Canadian Coalition Against Communism

Rukiye Turdush,
Uyghur Canadian Society, Former President

Interviewers from Happy Science[*]

Motohisa Fujii

Executive Director
Special Assistant to Religious Affairs Headquarters
Director General of International Politics Division

Mayumi Kobayashi

Manager of International Politics Division
Religious Affairs Headquarters

---

[*] Interviewers are listed in the order that they appear in the transcript.
Their professional titles represent their positions at the time of the interview.

1

Interviews with Three Activists

MC

Now, Master Ryuho Okawa will give us a lecture entitled, "Master Okawa's Answers to Canadian Activists." On October 6, after Master's Toronto lecture, "The Reason We Are Here," the International Politics Division interviewed Canadian activists to hear their comments. They asked us some questions.

So today, Master will give us answers to those questions. First, please watch the interview video.

[*Video footage of on-site interviews after the Toronto lecture*]

GLORIA FUNG

I feel very honored to be invited here to listen to Master Okawa's very enlightening lecture today because it has covered a lot of important topics in life—the importance of the intangible values of peace, love, happiness, and more importantly, the importance of the pursuit of Truth in life.

I'm also enlightened by his call for concern for people around the world in their struggle against totalitarianism. This is particularly important for people like myself, who was originally from Hong Kong, because the Hong Kong people are now at the very forefront of battlefield in China fighting for core values of human rights, freedom, rule of law, and democracy, which we Canadians as well as people around the world cherish dearly. So, this is not just about Hong Kong, it's also a Canadian and an international issue. I therefore concur with Master Okawa that all of us need to support the people of Hong Kong.

I would like to seek his advice as what the people of Canada and the international community could do to support the Hongkongers in their fight against totalitarian suppression from the Chinese Communist Party, how we can stay united and take concrete actions to make a positive change in this world.

SHENG XUE

I feel very honored to be here, and I'd like to say thank you to Master because he brought the very important message to Canada in his first lecture here. He also mentioned that China needs to be changed.

Happiness is the most important thing to every individual. I truly believe so. That's why we are having our life and come to this world. Everybody is trying to look for happiness, but only people who have freedom, human rights and democracy can truly enjoy happy lives. So, the whole world won't enjoy freedom and happiness until the 1.4 billion people in China are liberated from fear under the tyranny. This is a great task and a very important thing for everybody to think about. And Master has the ability so I would like to know his plan to help people in China to enjoy happiness one day, without fear and persecution from the Chinese tyranny.

Japan is becoming a great country, and is a democratic torch in Asia. I think Japan has the ability and responsibility to do more, especially to lead Asia for freedom and democracy. So, my question to Master is, "How can Japan do better and do more?" As he mentioned, related to the emergency situations in Hong Kong, the Japanese government doesn't do anything now, nor do other political parties; only Happiness Realization Party takes action, right? So, I really admire that a spiritual leader also can give comments on the real problems that we are facing today.

We need to enjoy freedom and human rights together, and have democracy as a political system of the country. But our world is far from perfect. Many people are living under fear and persecution, so they cannot enjoy happiness. I'd like to really contribute my life for more and more people to live with dignity.

I came from China, and I'm a Chinese-Canadian. That's why I do care more about people in China. I think this is the nature of human beings. Don't forget that there are 1.4 billion people in China. It's a huge amount of life there. They cannot enjoy freedom, human rights and democracy, which makes the world actually very dangerous. People there are being brainwashed and pressured, and are becoming the enemies of freedom. This is the urgent threat to the whole world. Everybody needs to take the responsibility to make a change, as Master said that China needs to be changed.

RUKIYE TURDUSH

Thank you very much for having me today. I feel so honored to participate in this event. This is my prestige. I am an Uyghur and immigrated to Canada 20 years ago and now I am the representative of Uyghurs.

I have a message for Master Ryuho Okawa, because he knows that more than three million Uyghur people in East Turkistan are suffering in the Chinese concentration camps. The Chinese empire colonized East Turkistan in 1949 and Uyghur people are living in open prison now.

What China is doing today is not only against the people but also it is against God because people in concentration camps are forced not to believe in Islam, and only to praise Xi Jinping and Chinese Communist Party. And they force people to transform their identity into Han Chinese. This is against God's will. God created diversity of people, but China declares war against God right now.

I think your organization's mission is to steer the power of people to fight against such evil regime to make a better world for the humanity. And we are willing to cooperate with you and the Hong Kong people to fight against the evil regime of Chinese Communist Party, and against any evil governments in this world. As people living in Canada, a democratic and free country, it is our prestige and unique responsibility to use this freedom to fight against evil.

As a Canadian, I would like to work together with you and my people will work with you too. Thank you very much for everything you have done. Your organization is the only one strong organization that can steer the power of people in grass root level as well as in government level, and make sure the people in the governments who are in power to do the right things.

As Master Ryuho Okawa said, the roots of all religions are one. Islam believes in only one God,

Allah, so there is no conflict with what Master said. The Jewish people believe in Elohim. Actually we say Elohim when we pray. We all have the same God. So, Elohim and Allah, and whatever the god's name may be, they are actually only one God. Whatever Master said has nothing to conflict with Islam. I'm happy with that.

It is people who changed things because of their own interests. Now we have to go back to the Truth. Like Master said, we have to unite as one and together with the power of the Creator we can change the world.

I would like Master Ryuho Okawa to mention Uyghur crisis in his speeches and lectures. He can raise awareness on what evil countries and governments are doing. What they're doing to Uyghur people is the fact and evidence. Many people don't know about China. Some people even say, "The Chinese government is a good government. They are not like American superpower and not going to invade other countries." I hope Master Ryuho Okawa raises Chinese issues so that people can understand the true color of China. Actually, no other regime is more evil than China.

2

Answer to Ms. Fung: Advice to Supporters of Hong Kong Democratic Protests

MC

Now, we will like to have a Q&A session with Master Okawa.

RYUHO OKAWA

OK. Is there anything you want to ask?

FUJII

Thank you for today. We'd like to ask you questions on behalf of three activists. Firstly, I will introduce their background and activities. And then, Ms. Kobayashi will add our relationship with the activists. Finally, she will ask you questions.

First person was a female activist, Ms. Gloria Fung, president of Canada-Hong Kong link. She is not just one of the most prominent activists in Canada, I believe she is the most famous and important activist in Canada against China's communist regime. And she is gathering e-petition, because now is the time for the federal election in Canada. She is engaging to raise awareness among Canadian politicians. Not only the Liberal Party and the Conservative Party, but all Canadian politicians should be aware of the Hong Kong issue. That's her mission now. We have relationship with her, so Ms. Kobayashi will explain about her.

KOBAYASHI

I met her for the first time in this May in Taiwan. She was attending as a representative from Canada to an event, which was to commemorate June 4th Tiananmen massacre. She had a very inspiring speech. So, I wanted her to come to our event as well. And when I invited her, she was very happy to attend the event because at that time her focus was on the e-petition that Mr. Fujii just said, she wanted to use this e-petition to push for Hong Kong to become Canadian federal election issue.

And I'd like to ask you a question on behalf of her. She was seeking for your advice on what Canadians as well as people around the world could do in order to support the Hong Kong people in the fight against dictatorial suppression.

China's strategy to change the opinion Of the world

RYUHO OKAWA

OK. They are very brave, I think, and they have conviction in their activities. It's good for them. I feel... the first person is Ms. Gloria Fung? She has power in her, of course, spiritual power, I felt. And her conviction is very strong. What she said will lead a lot of Canadian Chinese people. I think so.

But even in Canada, there are two groups. Generally speaking, one is acting for supporting Hong Kong, and another one is people who are protecting Beijing, China, including a lot of students from China. So, the Chinese society in Canada is not one. And I guess the number of the people who are living in Canada from mainland China is more than Hong Kong supporters. This is the strategy of Xi Jinping, China.

They have sent a lot of people all over the world, especially the key countries for them to change the opinion of the world. Of course, it's very difficult to change the opinion of the United States of America, but it's a little easier for them to change the opinion of Canada, Australia, New Zealand or weaker EU countries who are suffering from a revenue deficit. I mean, cannot-satisfy-their-people kind of country, for example, Greece or Italy or another one. They (China) are very strategic about that, so it's very difficult. And also, they have worldwide syndicates, so they are a very tough negotiator. I think so.

Of course, these people who are struggling against Beijing to help Hong Kong people have organizations worldwide, but they are very weak, I think, in the meaning of resources and in the meaning of their opinion and their resort, how to make influence on Chinese government. So, almost all of them are asking for help from other countries, especially from strong countries like G7. But their voices are not welcomed in every country.

But little by little, the supporters are getting more and more people assisting the problem of Hong Kong. For example, I already said in my lecture in Toronto, one Canadian military ship had passed near Hong Kong. It's one demonstration for Beijing China. And before this lecture, they caught the CFO of Huawei at the airport of Canada, and it's very helpful even for me to go to Canada. It means Canada is standing by the U.S. government. It means so. So, it's helpful for us to hold a lecture in Toronto.

Be patient, and continue to protest Using peaceful means

So, firstly I just want to say one thing. Of course, it's related to the second person, maybe. Xi Jinping's China is now thinking about separating what the Hong Kong government did and what Beijing China did, and their main strategy is to show the people of the world, all sorts of TV or newspapers writers, that this is just the confusion in Hong Kong and not the Beijing problem. This is the first strategy. I think so.

So, when I came back to Japan and read some opinion magazines of Japan, some conservative-trend magazine said that this—I mean, "this" means the Hong Kong demonstration-like thing—is like the old-fashioned Japanese students' rebellion against our government. It's my younger age. It's more than 50 years ago, around that. Someone says like that. The conservative people in Japan look at the matter of Hong Kong as a left-hand side activity, like the old-fashioned students' strike in universities in Japan and all around the world. They're thinking it's like that one. Another conservative opinion maker said that, "That is Asama Sansou Jiken (incident)," it means the Japanese Red Army's kidnapping and their fight against Japanese police and finally, they were perished by police. So, even the conservative side of Japanese opinionists is saying like that nowadays.

So, it will become the turning point, I think. I guess one is the petrol bomb, it's *kaen-bin* in Japanese. They say that a disguised policeman of Hong Kong did so, but when it broadcasted, people of the world, especially Japanese people, looked at that—one party is policemen shooting and attacking students or civilian people, but on another side, someone threw away the petrol bomb, so it's a not-so-good impression. So, if it's made by Beijing's hidden project, I think so, but it's not so good for the impression from that demonstration.

So, if they seek for freedom and democracy and peace, please be patient and keep a peaceful demonstration only. They can do, of course, walking or speaking or scattering their writings, it's OK, I think. But don't resist against the violence by violence. It's not so good. It will not get the compassion from other countries, especially the Japanese people who don't like struggle or trouble or conflict. So, be careful.

It's been more than 100 days. It's enough time. When there was the Tiananmen incident, Beijing didn't even have patience to keep silence and peace for 100 days. After that, there came a very important person from a foreign country. After that time, they did Tiananmen incident. So, it's a very difficult time, I think. To get the assistance from another country, don't show the conflict as the inner conflict of Hong Kong only.

Look at the situation from The objective view of an outside country

And I want to ask the demonstration people of Hong Kong, "Don't hate Hong Kong police or Hong Kong administration." They are also Hong Kong citizens. They are just obeying the order of Beijing, China, Xi Jinping regime. So, never hate the people of Hong Kong who are administrating, but please think, "This is just a problem of what they believe in or obey." This is a problem of system, and this is a problem of Marxism.

Even Xi Jinping is now spoken ill of regarding that he is wanting to replace the position of Mao Tse-tung, the founder of Chinese Communist Party. He is accused of that because (at the military parade in the 70th anniversary celebration) he rode on the same car which Mao Tse-tung used and no other person was in it (the following car). So, he was criticized that, "Xi Jinping is riding the same car with the ghost of Mao Tse-tung." He was said like that. So, the problem is very difficult.

Please look at the phenomenon from the viewpoint of other countries' people, I mean, objectively. It's very important. One illustration of that is, don't use petrol bomb. It's not good for the impression to other people of the world. Especially on TV occasion, it's not so good.

The world is following my design

How to destroy the Chinese government is a huge problem, indeed. This October 1, they made a great military march at the Tiananmen Square, and they showed the new ballistic missiles which can attack even the United States of America, and of course the aircraft carriers of the U.S. Such kind of new-type missiles, they showed. If we use forceful thinking, it will make the next war. So, think very cleverly.

My opinion is, I've been fighting against Xi Jinping during these almost 10 years. When he was the vice president of China, I saw that he's a very dangerous person. After he got his presidency, it came true, and I have been making a surrounding strategy for China. So, we made a good relationship with Donald Trump, the United States, and supported the victory of Republicans.

Also, we want to keep the good connections with Putin Russia, and of course, India, Nepal, Sri Lanka, the Philippines, Malaysia, Australia, and Europe. I have been surrounding Xi Jinping through my foreign activities, speeches, and lectures. I did a lot. And something's happened through my activities, for example, the policy of Australia or America. Canada is, just now. And I went to Germany. I'm making opinions of the world.

And through my mission, I have been giving opinion to our mass media. And Japan is also in the middle way now because we have a military alliance with the United States, but at the second time, we have an economic problem, so nothing strong deeds can be done by our government. They are just inviting the customers from Asian area, especially mainland China.

Japanese people cannot divide mainland China, Hong Kong, and Taiwan. But I think clearly, and in Taiwan this March, I said clearly what's the difference between mainland China and Taiwan, and in case of Hong Kong crisis, please help Hong Kong people. I asked Taiwanese people at that time. All are in my design and direction now.

A complicated strategy to surround China Through opinion and economy

But this fighting is a very huge one, so we need a surrounding strategy and we need, in the meaning of opinion, to surround Beijing China and criticize what is wrong. Its beginning is the one-party system of communism. It's the origin. And Xi Jinping is just aiming at being like Mao Tse-tung or China's First Emperor-like person. I published a lot of books regarding this matter, through Xi Jinping's guardian spirit's words.* So, Japanese people, including politics and the mass media, know a lot

---

* The author has already published a total of five books of spiritual interviews with the guardian spirit of Xi Jinping, including Hong Kong Revolution: Spiritual Messages of the Guardian Spirits of Xi Jinping and Agnes Chow Ting (Tokyo: HS Press, 2019) and Xi Jinping Shugorei Uyghur Dan'atsu wo Kataru (lit. "The Guardian Spirit of Xi Jinping Speaks on Suppression of Uyghurs," available in Japanese) (Tokyo: IRH Press, 2018).

from my books, but they can do nothing.

In addition to that, there was a tax hike on this October 1—it's the consumption tax, from eight percent to ten percent. Today is just 11 days after the tax hike, but today's newspaper reported that even the 7-Eleven chain stores are scheduled to close or relocate 1,000 stores. It's a huge one. And Sogo and Seibu departments, some of them are scheduled to close. It means, there comes the consumption depression.

Recently, we are weighted, so Mr. Prime Minister Abe must be just thinking about next year's Olympics, and at that time, he expects the economic growth of Japan again. So, Japanese government people and the opposite parties also don't work about this Hong Kong matter. Only we did and said a lot. It means we don't get votes from common people because to criticize gigantic China means inviting greater depressions for us.

So, we must overcome this problem. One should be to recognize that the hike of consumption tax was a failure. We repeatedly insisted that it's not time for us to raise consumption tax. Our economic growth is only one percent, or recently, only zero percent. If we made a raise of consumption tax, it would make our economy destroyed.

We have 2 times of governmental deficit compared to our total GDP, but Beijing China also has officially 2.5 times governmental deficit, or someone said 4 times government deficit, as much as their GDP. So, this is a chicken game: Japan or China, which is faster to be destroyed in the economic meaning? This is a very difficult game. I'm thinking about that.

China had made One Belt, One Road strategy. But it's at the verge of ruining now. I know about that. Mr. Kuroda, President of the Bank of Japan, made a great loan to developing countries, and he's making a competition with China's that kind of economic strategy. We are fighting in the level of economics and in the level of international monetary field. I'm suggesting a lot about that.

We have our political party, and Mr. Abe's plans are almost the same as what we dispatched. Only the tax hike was too early because of declining of the economy. So, we have also the same political problem. But maybe this is not their concern about their fighting.

We have a very complicated strategy, and are fighting in a lot of aspects; just, it's a surrounding strategy for China. It's a great strategy, so I said—I didn't say the name of the country, but I already said at the lecture of Toronto that I will finish the totalitarian regime of China from 2020 to 2030. It's our fighting for them. All of the Happy Science Group is concentrating on this problem. So, in the near future, we will overcome their ambition. I think so. Please rely on me about that.

Then, I just ask you for the repetition of the Hong Kong demonstration. Please be careful about that. Now, for example, just as I planned, the Uyghur people are scheduled to be protected by the U.S. government. I let them know a lot about that kind of great suffering. So, the future will be brighter. But it's another problem. I just want to say we'll do our best, and I will tell in every chance that I want to assist the Hong Kong people's freedom. But be careful acting. Never show your weak points to Beijing or other media. I hope so.

3

Answer to Ms. Sheng:
The Plan to Realize a Free China
Within the Next 10 Years

FUJII

Thank you for your precious advice for us and Ms. Gloria Fung. We will move on to the next question.

The second person was Ms. Sheng Xue, one of the prominent Chinese human rights activists and vice chairperson of the Federation for a Democratic China. For two years, we had a good relationship with her and her organization. At first, she visited our political party, Happiness Realization Party, during her visit to Japan two years ago, and we have been keeping in touch. Then, this time, it was her first time to attend Master's event, so she was very pleased to join it. As you told us in your lecture (entitled "What I thought in Canada") yesterday, she invited Ms. Kobayashi the night before the event.

RYUHO OKAWA

Oh, yeah, brave. She's brave.

FUJII

[*Laughs.*] Yes, she had a dinner with them. She will explain about that.

KOBAYASHI

A lot of Chinese activists gathered at her place, and they had a discussion on the unity of groups to fight against the Chinese Communist Party's tyranny. Her house was like a shelter for people who have fled to Canada. So, once they arrive in Toronto, they will go to her house, so that they have a place to stay. I think she is a very loving person to protect all the people who have escaped from China.

I asked them, "Which party in Canada do you support? Conservative Party of Canada or The Liberal Party?" and their answer was, "Conservative Party." I asked the reason why, and they said that, "Because Prime Minister Trudeau doesn't have any idea for Chinese issues." And his father, Pierre Trudeau, was so pro-China. So, they said, "He just wants to do something that his father did." That's why they couldn't support him.

And they're hoping that, if the Conservative Party wins in the coming election, the relationship between Canada and the United States would become much closer. That means Canada will follow President Trump's Chinese policies. That's the reason why they supported the Conservative Party. We had a great discussion. Also, they hoped your lecture to be very successful, so we made a wish together for the success of your event on the following day. So, may I ask you her questions?

RYUHO OKAWA

Uh huh.

KOBAYASHI

She had two questions. First, she wanted to know about Master's plan for Chinese people to enjoy happiness and freedom without persecution from Chinese Communist Party. A lot of people are suffering, as she said, so she would like you to tell us your plan to set them free.

And the second question was, you talked a little about it (in the lecture in Toronto), but she thinks that Japan is a great nation. She used the words, "a democratic torch in Asia." She had great expectations for Japan. But she feels like what Japan does is not enough. So, she was willing to ask you how Japan can do better and give more effort to fulfill its mission.

Canada should adopt
The Benjamin Franklin spirit

RYUHO OKAWA

OK. It's also a very difficult problem. Maybe it's beyond their power today. I hope also for the victory of Conservative Party of Canada. It's Mr. Scheer's victory. If we can get such victory, there is a conservative line: Boris Johnson and Mr. Scheer and Donald Trump. These three guys are very powerful on the communist party. I think so.

I had a plan to realize that. But our followers in Toronto, or Canada, are not so great, so in the election meaning, we don't have enough power for that. So, I just want to say the mistakes of Prime Minister Trudeau. We can criticize about that, and it's good for Mr. Scheer to become the next prime minister. He is powerful now. Mr. Trudeau changed his political attitude these days, but Mr. Trudeau is still strong in Canada, so we need another "God's wind" like when we experienced Donald Trump's victory.

Canada's weak point, I already told about that. Mr. Trudeau likes to be liberal, it's from his father. But to be liberal does not mean to be democratic. Democracy is not always liberal. In these times, in the United States also, Canada also, and other European countries, "liberal" means sometimes a labor party- or communist-like thinking.

So, we must stop "liberal" to some extent, and change it to the direction of how to make their country stronger in the meaning of liberal. It's a Benjamin Franklin spirit, I think. In the meaning of Benjamin Franklin's spirit, to be liberal is good, but if we use "liberal" to save people by dint of government's power only—give money, scattering money only, or buy votes by scattering money—this "liberal" leads to hell. I want to say so.

Mr. Trudeau's father is not a god. I also want to add it. Canada is a good country, but its diversity and its tolerance are enough, and over-enough, indeed. If it's combined with too much liberal, it means Canada will be led to communist party-like country, or Sweden-like country in the meaning of environmentalists. It's almost the same.

A long timespan of planning
To change the Earth

It was told that there is a 16-year-old lady who insists on environments and global warming. She was supported by two groups, one of which is assisted by Chinese money, I've heard. So, it's the strategy of Xi Jinping China. He uses environment and global warming. In China, there are very much emissions of CO_2 through their coal-powered electricity, but it's a hidden part. They just want to weaken Donald

Trump's America First policy. That's their aim. So, Chinese government uses only, a 16-year-old, just a small girl. It's their way.

I said that (problem of) environment is quite different. I said Donald Trump is true. CO_2 emission does not have strong influence on us. If you want to stop all the CO_2 by 2050, please save the poverty of the people instead. They need food, they need industry. It's important. I said so.

Global warming is not the only reason of this Earth's climate. I know a lot about that. We have designed the long timespan of planning to change this Earth and how to make civilization prosper on this Earth. So, what she said is not right. I said so.

But Canadian people like environment. They like beaver, they like reindeer, like that. So, they are living in heaven with animals, maybe heavenly animals. So, my wife said when we visited Canada, "They need sixth dimensional world and seventh dimensional world in Canada." We could see only fourth dimensional world and fifth dimensional world. Where is the sixth dimensional world, where is the seventh dimensional world, or where is the eighth dimensional world in the air of Canada? We could not find anyone in that area like Australia when we visited it. We could not see anyone in that area because they have only 200 years or so, very short history.

So, I said there is no god in some meaning because of course, the ancient worldwide God is watching them, but Mr. Trudeau's father is not a god, of course. Alexander Wood is also not a god. So, I want our Happy Science Canadian members to become a greater person and make the world of angels in the heaven of Canada. I hope so.

And, our fighting way is to change policy of Mr. Trudeau and to assist Mr. Scheer. Even if we fail in this election—it's only 10 more days, so it's not enough, I think, but our activities will change

Canada in the near future. And Mr. Trudeau also will change his mind; if it's bad or it's not so effective, he will change his mind. This is the political activities in Canada, we hope so.

The danger of a surveillance society Ruled by AI

RYUHO OKAWA

And she asked me the plan? How to dissolve China?

KOBAYASHI

Yes, your plan to liberate, to make Chinese people enjoy freedom and happiness.

RYUHO OKAWA

Ah, it's a great problem, but the end is coming, I think. People, I mean even the people of

Communists are hating the one-party system and Xi Jinping's dictatorship. As you know, there are a lot of cameras which are surveying the people, surveillance cameras, and these become 600 million cameras next year, I mean 2020. 1.4 billion people are watched by 0.6 billion cameras means two people are watched by one camera, almost. No one can think about such kind of *1984*-like, George Orwell's telescreen society. It's a society of fear; fearful society came again.

The real god of China is AI. AI can decide almost everything. It's very fearful. So, we can make such kind of opinion: If people want to be free, we don't need any cameras watching us, or don't need to check every person's money's working through the electronic system. Just the controlling is everything. It's also a fearful future.

So, someone must say about another George Orwell-like warning to them. They think that, "We are a very advanced country because we can use AI and we can make slave our 1.4 billion people through AI system," but it's not good for fundamental human rights. To be free is, you can be free to think about and to walk about and to choose anything.

So, our next project is to make collapse within them by dint of our thinking or thought. "Are you happy or not?" We'll ask them and change them. Chinese people will come to Japan, but at that time, we can ask them and influence them. "Are you really happy in your society? Is this a human society or the society of happiness? If not, you should change it. If not, it's because of the difference of aim of your country. Your head of the country is just aiming at controlling people. Just controlling people means peaceful for government-side person, but common people are not happy and peaceful."

It's like the Nazism-like society. It's like the Lenin- and Stalin-like regime's style. Chinese people are not the Jewish people who were killed by Hitler. Xi Jinping is now a new Hitler who can kill 1.4 billion people. If they don't obey his order, he can kill everyone. And he is also controlling the opinion or the communication of every person through a lot of intelligent police. Hundreds of thousands of people are working for intelligence police. And to criticize the system will ruin their regime, I think. I already told them at the Toronto lecture that one is mass murder, second is the secret police, and the third is a concentration camp. These are the characteristic points of a totalitarian regime, a dictatorship regime like Hitler or Stalin, I already said so in Taiwan. So, it's a battle of thinking, a battle of opinion.

Above economy and politics
Lies God's justice

So, Japanese people, just stop thinking about money or income only. We must think about politics. And above politics, there is God's justice! This is what Happy Science is teaching Japanese people. Japanese people or Japanese government think about economy and income and money only. We were told that Japanese are "economic animals" before we experienced the great depression through 1990's. We are told that Japanese are economic animals. Now, still, its criticism can survive if we cannot change our mind. We must seek for world justice, God's justice, and have responsibility. It's very important.

I saw almost the same thing in Canada. Canada has some kind of freedom and tolerance, indeed, but I felt a little responsibility. Of course, they think, "We are a not-so-large country and have a not-so-large population, so we don't have enough power worldwide." They should think so, but it's the same in Japan also. Canada and Japan also, we belong to G7, and we must have responsibility and want to say something to China who does not belong to G7.

The United Nations permanent members are five countries: The United States of America, the U.K., France, China, and Russia. China and Russia are always the problem. So, we must remake this system also. It was just active at the end of World War II, but now it's not active, it's not effective. We must change this UN. Japan has been the No.1 or No.2 country of "happiness planting" (contribution) for the UN, but we don't have enough opinion to speak to them. So, we must say something to the UN. If they won't receive our opinions, we don't support them in the meaning of budget. We must be a politician in this meaning and must be stronger than we used to be. So, these things I'm thinking about.

In this meaning, we, Happy Science, need a lot of members, more members, and more branches all over the world, and of course, have more power in Japan also. But our age will come in the near future. We will change the world, next 10 years. It's my answer.

4

Answer to Ms. Turdush: A Message to Fighters Who Have Faith in God

FUJII

Then we are moving on to the third person. She is Rukiye Turdush, former president of Canadian Uyghur Society. She is an enthusiastic activist. A few years ago, she found Master's book online. She already read *Into the Storm of International Politics* (see p.213) and told us that Master is great and she is big fan of Master. Her impression of the book was, "Master's view on world affair is very clear and to the point." She is very close to our team. Ms. Kobayashi will explain our relation with her.

KOBAYASHI

Yes. On the next day, she invited me to her house. It's two hours' drive. That means she drove two hours to attend your lecture. And she said, after she read the book *Into the Storm of International Politics*, she was very impressed. Even though she missed your lecture in New York, she was thinking to herself that if you, Master, ever come back to New York, she was willing to attend from Canada to New York, just for your lecture. So, when I invited her to the event, she was super happy and decided to attend on the spot. She was looking forward to your visit for a long time.

FUJII

This February, she was invited to an event at McMaster University as a speaker. But some student protesters from China interrupted her. It was a kind of incident, so even the U.S. media covered it. So, she is very famous for her anti-communism activity as an Uyghur.

KOBAYASHI

It showed that there are so many Chinese student groups in Canada, which are against those activists. So, all those three people are really fighting against Chinese Communist Party in spite of repeated interference from those groups.

Her question was that, a lot of Uyghur people as well as Tibetans, Inner-Mongolians, and Christians in underground churches are suffering under severe oppression. They are losing hope because of the oppression. But she believes that no devil can defeat God. She believes that she's always on the winning side as long as she's with God, so she has very strong faith in God. Could you please give your message to those fighters who have faith in God? Thank you.

The world is now changing
After I gave lectures in Germany and Taiwan

RYUHO OKAWA

OK, OK, OK. Ms. Rukiye Turdush who came from Uyghur. Yes, I'm very much impressed from her interview. She is a religious person, so I also was moved by her voice. She said, "Allah and Elohim are the same. And we sometimes pray for Elohim," she said. It's a good point.

I firstly heard about the problem of Uyghur last summer, not this year, but the previous year's end of the summer or September. Activists of Uyghur problem came to our Happiness Realization Party and said that, "We asked Prime Minister Abe or around him about the problem of Uyghur, but Mr. Abe or the LDP, Liberal Democratic Party, did nothing. So, we need help of Master Ryuho Okawa." I've heard that, so I made a lecture last October in Germany and I firstly referred to East

Turkistan problem—formally, it's East Turkistan problem, but almost all Japanese don't know about that, so "Uyghur problem".

There are millions of people who are suffering from the persecution from Beijing, China, like the Jewish people were done from Adolf Hitler. I said so. After last October's lecture, two or three days later, China's government admitted that there was a concentration camp of Uyghur people. They formally admitted that. But at that time, they said, "We are just educating. Educating because, Uyghur people, if they are educated through their own culture only, they cannot get jobs from other Chinese companies, and they cannot enter the universities of China. So, we want to change their education and teach them Chinese, and in addition, to train how to behave like Chinese." They said so. But they admitted to the concentration camp.

I referred to this problem again, this March, in my Taiwan lecture, and at that time, also, I referred to Hong Kong problem. "Taiwan should be Taiwan. 'One country, two systems' doesn't work. So, please keep your freedom, democracy, and prosperity," I said to them. At that time, Tsai Ing-wen had a lesser power, but now, she recovered again, and she will win in the next election. I hope so. Its starting point was my lecture. And, at that time, I also said that, "Please help Hong Kong people. If they are in trouble, please help them." I said so. Now, Taiwan people are assisting Hong Kong people, indeed. To protect Hong Kong means to protect Taiwan. To protect Taiwan means to protect Japan, and to protect the Philippines or Vietnam or other countries.

Xi Jinping is now traveling around India and Nepal because of trading problem with the United

States of America. He wants to make a new way for their trading system. But in these countries already I made a lecture, so they will not change their mind in the main concept. So, we will continue the surrounding-China strategy, continuously.

The end of China: its economic collapse

And I will collapse the economy of Communist Party. It is said that, if the economic growth were less than seven percent, the one-party system will be collapsed. I've heard so. Now, they are around six percent economic growth, but this is just a lie. Their development speed is lower than this one, almost the same as Japan or so. So, people will know the reality of their economics.

In the country of China, "What God is" means economic growth. They had been making a great economic growth through these 30 years. This is their religion. This is their faith. Their faith in communism or socialist system is better than American way of capitalism or Japanese way of system. But Mr. Donald Trump already found what happened in these 30 years. And in Japan also, I already found what happened to China and what happened to Japan. I already told a lot about that. It was American policy to help China and make Japan lose, but they changed their mind. They will assist Japanese economy and they will want to ruin Chinese economy. This is the next decade, I surely said so.

So, they will suffer a worldwide ruin. One Belt, One Road system will be ruined in the near future, and I will, we will ruin them. In this context, "we" includes our Happiness Realization Party; we must make the next strategy for Japanese economic growth, and we must again get the No.2 of the economic level. At that time, it will be the end of communist one-party system, the end of China. I think so. We have such kind of strategy.

Elohim's promise to His people of Uyghur

RYUHO OKAWA

And this Ms. Rukiye Turdush, she had a deep faith in God. I'll answer her.

> This is the voice of Elohim, Your God.
> Your Uyghur people's God is here in Japan!
> So, I will save you.
> I will save you.
>
> This is the promise of God!
> So, please believe in me!
> I will set you free in the near future!

I will do my best,
We will do our best,
And you can continue
Your faith in God.
You will be safe.
I hope so,
I want to do so,
And I will save you.

KOBAYASHI

Thank you so much for your great message. We will make sure that your message will be heard by every single person. Thank you so much.

5

God's Plan and Our Mission

FUJII

Thank you for your precious answers to the questions. Lastly, just for your information. On Tuesday this week, it means just two days after the Toronto event, BBC, one of the major TV networks, offered to broadcast *Reigen* (spiritual message) from Margaret Thatcher.[*]

RYUHO OKAWA

Margaret Thatcher... OK.

FUJII

They asked it to our London *shibucho* (branch manager). She succeeded in promoting Reigen in

---

* Here, he is referring to the spiritual messages from Thatcher given on April 9, 2013, just 19 hours after her death. See Ryuho Okawa, Margaret Thatcher's Miraculous Message: An Interview with the Iron Lady 19 Hours After Her Death (Tokyo: HS Press, 2013).

London. This is very precious information, because I think it means Master made a huge impact in Toronto. So, every British media knows that. I believe so.

RYUHO OKAWA

Ah, really? OK. I appreciate it. Yes, we need a new message from Margaret Thatcher or Winston Churchill or the guardian spirit of Boris Johnson in the near future. Next strategy for London or New York, we must make some plan for that.

I'll add that I already predicted the birth of President Mr. Donald Trump in the year of 1989 in my book, *Invincible Thinking* (see p.213). Almost 30 years ago, firstly. Second is, January of 2016, and next is the autumn, one month before the general election. I predicted the victory of Donald Trump in New York lecture. Even our followers said, "Oh, Master, you should never have said so. We are convinced that Mrs. Clinton will win. It's already fixed, so it's a mistake." They said, but Donald Trump won. It's God's plan.

So, he is required because of the fight against China. He is wanted to fight against China, and we, also, have such kind of mission. So, the future will be brighter. I want to say so. Thank you very much.

Translator's note: Chapter 4 was originally recorded in Japanese, and later translated into English.

4

Spiritual Messages from God Thoth:

God of North America
speaks His mind

Recorded October 5, 2019 in Canada

Thoth (About 12,000 years ago)

The great religious master who led the Atlantis civilization to its golden age. He was a super genius who was a religious leader, politician, philosopher, scientist, and artist all in one. Also called the Omniscient and Omnipotent Lord Thoth. Thoth is a (ninth-dimensional) branch spirit of El Cantare, God of the Earth, and is also known as an ancient Egyptian god. See Ryuho Okawa, *The Laws of the Sun* (New York: IRH Press, 2018), and *The Mystical Laws* (Tokyo: HS Press, 2015).

Interviewers from Happy Science[*]

Shio Okawa
Aide to Master & CEO

Sakurako Jimmu
Managing Director
Chief Secretary of First Secretarial Division
Religious Affairs Headquarters

The opinions of the spirit do not necessarily reflect those of Happy Science Group.
For the mechanism behind spiritual messages, see end section.

1

Summoning Thoth,
God of North America,
Before the Canada Lecture

RYUHO OKAWA

Thoth, God of North America.*

Thoth, God of North America.

O Thoth, God of North America.

Before tomorrow's lecture

(In Toronto, Canada. See Chapter 1),

We wish to hear your final opinion.

O God Thoth, God of North America,

Who is mainly guiding North America.

Before tomorrow's lecture,

We wish to hear your conclusion.

Please give us your guidance.

[*Five seconds of silence.*]

---

* See Chapter 2.

GOD THOTH

Yes.

SHIO OKAWA

Thank you always for your guidance.

GOD THOTH

Yes.

SHIO OKAWA

For tomorrow's lecture in Canada, there are four points I wish to ask you.

GOD THOTH

Yes.

2

On Global Warming

Increase in CO$_2$ leads to
More greens and new agriculture

SHIO OKAWA

First question is about global warming. Canada seems to have strong interests in the environmental issues. Also, Ms. Greta Thunberg took part in some activities here. A short while ago, we have also asked God Odin about this issue and he said "it is a destiny." And he also mentioned that "humans should not involve themselves too much about producing or reducing CO$_2$. To a certain degree, there are plans for the land to shift on a global scale that could cause some parts to sink and other parts to rise. That is beyond what humans can control." That was his answer, how about you, God Thoth? What do you think about this issue?

GOD THOTH

In regards to CO_2, when you look at the history of Earth, there used to be a lot more CO_2. In short, it was not the matter of man-made automobiles and their gas emissions, but it was due to volcanic eruptions generating far more CO_2.

SHIO OKAWA

I see.

GOD THOTH

Skies were covered with clouds of carbon dioxide in some era. Compared with that, skies nowadays are very clean and most of the CO_2 is now turned into the green foliage of the forests. In fact, CO_2 is the source of nutrition of plants. Plants converts CO_2 by carbon dioxide assimilation to produce oxygen.

SHIO OKAWA

You are right.

GOD THOTH

When the CO_2 concentration rises, Earth may seem to warm up temporarily. The increase in the temperature means increase in nutrients for plants and that means they flourish which in turn produce more oxygen. As a result, there will be potentials for new agriculture and resources. CO_2 has increased quite rapidly over the past century for sure, but from a long historical standpoint, it is far less than the level produced by volcanic eruptions comparatively.

SHIO OKAWA

I agree.

GOD THOTH

The amount of CO_2 produced on earth currently is much less than, for example, the clouds of CO_2 that covered the earth when the volcanic mountain Vesuvius of Pompei erupted. Those numbers relating to CO_2 must have been calculated by the number crunchers, most likely, but natural self-purification system will work itself out, so it is not a matter to be concerned about.

SHIO OKAWA
Earth itself will perform self-purification.

GOD THOTH
Certainly.

SHIO OKAWA
It could change weather patterns.

GOD THOTH
What is now the desert region could next be the green land for agricultural use instead.

SHIO OKAWA
I understand.

GOD THOTH

People may believe that more people produce more CO_2, but that may not be a bad thing because more CO_2 helps increase the green belt in areas such as the large desert regions in Africa, Middle East and in Australia. Even in the tundra region of Russia could see increase in greener areas. So, it's not a bad thing overall, I think. To give you my conclusion, Mr. Trump is right. (Editorial note: President Trump has been skeptical of the correlation between the climate change and CO_2 and has taken a prudent stance on regulating CO_2 emission.)

SHIO OKAWA

Both Mr. Trump and Mr. Putin?

GOD THOTH

Yes.

SHIO OKAWA

I see.

"Return to nature movement"
Leads to left-wing Marxism

SHIO OKAWA

Current environmental activities against global warming often claim to "Believe in Science."

GOD THOTH

I think they want to deny all the achievements after the Industrial Revolution. This is some kind of "return to nature movement" like Rousseau said and it leads to the left-wing stance.

SHIO OKAWA

After all, it is scientific progress that is causing all kinds of emissions (such as CO_2 that environmental activists fear).

GOD THOTH

Yes, it certainly leads to the left-wing Marxism. One of the problems of Marxism is not understanding the improved productivity. They say how emission of CO_2 will lead to our doom but they are overlooking the fact that increasing productivity will enhance the overall convenience and create added value which helps increase income level for many people and encourages increase in food productions. They are neglecting to acknowledge this cycle and it is scientifically wrong.

SHIO OKAWA
Indeed.

More rain and CO_2 will make deserts greener

JIMMU
Now the world population is heading 10 billion, and there is talk of impending food crisis. Can we consider global warming as some kind of mercy to prevent that crisis?

GOD THOTH

Africa used to be a lot greener long time ago, and yet desertification continues to advance. Therefore, having more rain and CO_2 will make it easier to reverse its course and grow greener once again.

SHIO OKAWA

Most certainly.

GOD THOTH

There will be ample greenery.

SHIO OKAWA

Right now, African animals are facing a crisis because of disappearing of forests.

GOD THOTH

Yes, there are only shrubs and withering trees growing only sparsely.

SHIO OKAWA

Yes, it is so.

GOD THOTH

Animals are losing their food source and limited number of animals are being eaten by humans and dying out, so increase of CO_2 should be a welcome news. Developed nations are producing CO_2, and the effect could turn undeveloped area such as Africa or Gobi Desert into greener land. If you try to use solar energy alone, reduced CO_2 level will adversely promote more desertification.

SHIO OKAWA

Does that mean that if you oppose global warming to an extreme, that path will lead to the direction of dwindling population of humans and animals alike?

GOD THOTH

In fact, it is "global perishing."

SHIO OKAWA

I see.

GOD THOTH

It will lead towards that direction. People are making an issue of melting glaciers, but they are turning into water, and eventually when the seawater temperature rises to cause evaporation of water, it becomes rain clouds and drops rain back down to earth. Then, it will help grow vegetations and help create forests. In other words, forests can be created from rain and CO_2.

SHIO OKAWA

I understand.

GOD THOTH

Therefore, based on science, Ms. Greta Thunberg's claims are wrong.

SHIO OKAWA

Yes.

JIMMU

Thank you very much.

3

How Will the Hong Kong Revolution Turn Out?

JIMMU

Next, I'd like to ask you about China and Hong Kong. The Hong Kong Revolution is going on now, and according to today's news, the anti-mask law was passed in Hong Kong. As you can see, the Hong Kong Revolution that seeks for more freedom and the Xi Jinping regime are clashing against each other. What kind of future do you see from all this?

GOD THOTH

In short, Xi Jinping wants to make the Hong Kong people hate Chief Executive Carrie Lam. Of course.

SHIO OKAWA

I see.

GOD THOTH

He is trying to make them hate her and the police, so that the issue becomes a conflict within Hong Kong. That's why he had her make a law to ban masks. People on Xi Jinping's side are trying to keep themselves safe.

China says they guarantee "one country, two systems" policy, but they are trying to have the international community recognize the matter as just a struggle within Hong Kong. But the international community is criticizing them a lot.

Even if the Hong Kong police make violence, they can say it's just a public disorder in Hong Kong. In the end, the Xi Jinping regime will solve the problem by removing the chief executive. They want to do so.

You asked me about the future, and hmm... [*About 10 seconds of silence.*] The future I predict is that, "(China's regime will be) Upside down in the next 10 years." I think so.

SHIO OKAWA

You mean, the Hong Kong people enjoying freedom now will become the majority?

GOD THOTH

Yes. Even though China says they are a communist country, they enjoy prosperity by capitalism and liberalism in the economic meaning, and practice communism in the political meaning. But if they keep the status quo in their politics, their economy will decline. That will be the next age. They will slow down.

If there is no freedom in politics, there will be no freedom in economy. This is natural, and this will be proved naturally in the next age, so the Xi Jinping regime will fall.

SHIO OKAWA

You're right. If people become more wealthy in the economic meaning, that will not be compatible with communism.

GOD THOTH

China thinks that Deng Xiaoping succeeded in preventing China from Soviet-like collapse by giving freedom to economy, but keeping the status quo in politics. So, they are trying to keep that way.

China combined the two systems to make one system called modified socialism, and think they are practicing that. But Hong Kong is proving that if there is no freedom in politics, there will be no freedom in economy, so in the end, there will be more freedom in mainland China.

So, the regime now will surely be defeated. Why? Because the credibility of the communist government now depends on its economic progress.

SHIO OKAWA

Ah.

GOD THOTH

So, if economic progress stops, there will be nothing to believe in.

SHIO OKAWA

I see.

GOD THOTH

In China, only the economic growth rate is the substitute for God. When the economic growth stops, at that time, China will fall. So, they will have no choice but to introduce freedom.

What will happen after that? It's been a long time, but they will shift to a parliamentary democracy. I think so.

SHIO OKAWA

OK.

GOD THOTH

They will have to adopt democracy, which they hate.

If Carrie Lam or the head of police or people like that don't die in the inner conflict, the Beijing government will blame them and fire them as a symbol of reconciliation, maybe. I think so.

SHIO OKAWA

In mainland China, it's illegal to participate in a protest and to criticize the regime on SNS. Now, in Hong Kong, the government is trying to pass a law that prevents people from wearing masks. If they wear masks, they can be arrested, I think.

GOD THOTH

Ah, that won't happen. People will start destroying the surveillance cameras soon.

SHIO OKAWA

I see [*laughs*].

GOD THOTH

They will destroy the cameras one by one. They can easily destroy the cameras.

SHIO OKAWA

It seems like the Hong Kong government is now trying to apply Chinese law to Hong Kong.

GOD THOTH

They think China is advanced, but the people are denying a future society ruled by AI (artificial intelligence). The Hong Kong government is trying to make another totalitarian society using a different way, but the people are denying it. So, the truth is that the government will lose.

SHIO OKAWA

I read a book on the surveillance system in China. Now, it's really like a society where people are tagged and controlled.

GOD THOTH

And, the authorities themselves are watched, also.

SHIO OKAWA

Ah, you're right.

GOD THOTH

So, they will be defeated when their own secret information is revealed.

SHIO OKAWA

I see.

GOD THOTH

They will be defeated because people will find out a lot of things that they are doing. They won't last another 10 years.

So, support the Hong Kong Revolution and support the activists overseas. That is the right direction. I think so.

The Chinese government uses the word "riot" to explain the Hong Kong situation, but there have been about 100,000 riots a year in Uyghur, Tibet, and Inner Mongolia. It's just that people don't know because these are not broadcasted or reported. The one in Hong Kong is called a riot, also, right? The insisting of human rights as a group, for example, protests or political movements, the Chinese government calls them riots.

So, the democratic movement has been going on for the last 10 or 20 years already. It's been going on from the Tiananmen (Incident), and now, the movement is showing up on the surface. China will collapse from the south part. I think so.

SHIO OKAWA
OK.

GOD THOTH
And, I think there will come revolutionaries from

inside the Chinese Communist Party. Hmm, a collapse. There is no other way. Definitely. One hundred percent. They will collapse.

SHIO OKAWA

OK. I understand.

4

LGBT in the Eyes of God Thoth

LGBT is an insect-like or animal-like value That rejects God's eyes

SHIO OKAWA

Next is Canada's LGBT issue. What do you think of this problem?

GOD THOTH

[*Sighs.*] They are some kind of... how do I say, they do not recognize the existence of souls or heaven and hell. In other words, this world is everything to them. They believe happiness means being able to do whatever they want. They do not recognize that there is the world that comes after and that God is watching. I think so.

In some meaning, this leads to some kind of atheism. I guess so. They are ignoring the eyes of God. But the God of the Earth created this Earth based on relativity. For now, that is the policy on Earth.

As you said, a world of one sex is like the world of insects. Humans are advanced beings because men and women were separated, and they make progress by polishing each other and finding their best match.

But if they need to make children only, they can just lay eggs. They don't need courtship or like that. That is an insect-like value. Maybe it is an animal-like value. Animals and insects don't think about the other world. I think so. So, it means they have no fear of God. It's the modern-day Sodom and Gomorrah, so they will be destroyed. After freedom, there comes heavy suppression.

SHIO OKAWA
Ah.

GOD THOTH

LGBT will be made lawful and free all around the world, and after that, there will occur Sodom and Gomorrah. God's anger will be realized in another way.

Same-sex love is another form of materialism, And disobedience to God

SHIO OKAWA

Some people cannot help but be attracted to the same sex. What kind of advice would you give them? In some cases, a male soul might be in a female body, or a male soul is possessing a living female. Or, maybe two people of the same sex now was a husband and a wife in their previous life, or many other cases like that.

GOD THOTH

Basically, they don't recognize spiritual values. They are another form of materialism, I think. They are hedonists who feels pleasure and thrill in the physical contact between man and man, or woman and woman. They are not spiritual or mentally developed. I mean, religions have commandments and teachings on what is good and what is bad, but such people say it's not their problem. For example, imagine a world where people think they can do what they want to do as long as they do not kill anyone. It's a world like that. They think what they want to do is justice.

SHIO OKAWA

What if they fall in love mentally?

GOD THOTH

It means they have a disease. It is the disease of the soul. I think so.

SHIO OKAWA

I see.

GOD THOTH

Humans were not made like that.

SHIO OKAWA

So, it means God has a clear idea of how humans should be, right?

GOD THOTH

They are disobeying God. They were born as a woman or a man, but are objecting to that. However, they cannot do that because they agreed to the plan to be born as a woman or a man, before they were born.

SHIO OKAWA

I see.

GOD THOTH

They were born under such kind of condition, but they are hating heaven, their parents, and their society. They are saying to let them do what they want.

Spread LGBT,
And there will come new suppression

GOD THOTH

Their way of life is not so good for a healthy society. Now, LGBT people are getting more freedom, and they think that spreading LGBT or rainbow is a good thing because it means liberty, but this is like the French Revolution. After the liberty, there comes not the guillotine, but comes Reign of Terror. I think so.

Like the Red Scare, there will occur the LGBT Scare in the near future. It will occur after LGBT spreads a little more. But you should prepare for it already. How much right can we give to materialistic and atheistic hedonists who ignore God, Buddha, religion, or ethics and morals? Such kind of world is a very small, hidden world. They are having fun living that way because they live in secret. But when they come out in the open world, they will be "struck by lightning." So, there will occur new suppression, another kind of suppression different from totalitarianism. LGBT is not allowed because human beings have the desire to keep living on Earth for hundreds of millions of years more.

There is materialistic thinking behind LGBT

SHIO OKAWA

So, you mean, we shouldn't forget that humans exist because God allows us to live, right?

GOD THOTH

They are protesting about their own sex, and in their opinion is a materialistic view that life can be created in a test tube.

SHIO OKAWA

Human life?

GOD THOTH

Yeah, yeah. They are wrong about that. Before you are born, each of you choose your own parents and decide to be born as male or female, and make a rough plan of your life. People who are dissatisfied of their own plan might turn to LGBT, commit suicide, or cause their own downfall, like criminals. Nobody lives to destroy their family, but they end up doing that.

The good part of Kant's philosophy was that he said, "What would happen if everyone does what you did? If it is good for everyone else, do it, but if it is not good, don't do it." This is what he means by maxim. It means the morals of a right human being. If the LGBT population is at a low percentage, around 0.8, it is the limit for them to live happily. I guess so. But if everyone in society seeks for it, then they don't deserve to be protected. They will be persecuted. When more than 20 to 30 percent of people seek for it, they will be suppressed. I think so. They will experience more tough times. There will come a different kind of Hitler, another kind.

God's rule that humans cannot change

GOD THOTH

And, we don't know what happens to transsexual people until they die.

SHIO OKAWA

Everyone picks his or her assignment for this life and chooses their sex, male or female, before being born.

GOD THOTH

It is for several decades only.

SHIO OKAWA

They must think from that standpoint.

GOD THOTH

You will know why you were born as your sex and into your family when you return to the other world. You forget how you were before you came to this world because that is the rule. God made this rule, so you cannot change it. This world is complete by itself, you might think so, but you have to realize that it is not true. That is the reason there are religions. LGBT defies religion or makes religion weaker, in some meaning.

SHIO OKAWA

You're right.

GOD THOTH

Right now, it's no problem for them, it might be so. But when there are more and more LGBT people, at that time, surely, they will be suppressed.

SHIO OKAWA

As you said, we have to recall the viewpoint that we, humans, were created by God, and think about why God created us this way.

GOD THOTH

God is against totalitarianism that makes people slaves, and He will also punish arrogant people who falsely believe that they can bind God.

SHIO OKAWA

Freddie Mercury's song, "We Are The Champions"...

GOD THOTH

Wrong.

SHIO OKAWA

Wrong. OK.

GOD THOTH

A human has become God. A lot of people, 300,000 people gathered and cheered for him, and now he thinks he is God. But he is wrong.

SHIO OKAWA

Yes.

GOD THOTH

He is wrong. He thinks it's an age of "no God."

SHIO OKAWA

He is thinking, "A human can live as he wants. What's wrong with that?"

GOD THOTH

Being selfish and being free are not the same thing. Real freedom is accompanied by responsibility.

The truth about Oscar Wilde

JIMMU

Recently, we recorded the spiritual messages from Oscar Wilde. (Recorded on August 30, 2019. See *Spiritual Messages from Oscar Wilde: Love, Beauty, and LGBT* [Tokyo: HS Press, 2019].) Usually, when we receive spiritual messages from people who were LGBT, most of them are in hell, but Oscar Wilde was a holy spirit in heaven.

GOD THOTH

Yes.

JIMMU

This made the matter complicated, and we are confused. What divides heaven and hell for LGBT people?

GOD THOTH

Oscar Wilde was not just about LGBT. At the time, the British aristocrats were corrupt, and the British society was going through a changing period. He wrote something sexual, but in reality, he was trying to convey the problems of corruption in aristocracy.

SHIO OKAWA

So, that is why he wrote *The Picture of Dorian Gray*.

GOD THOTH

Yes, yes, he wanted to say that. He wanted to say about the corruption of aristocrats. It was the introduction to the democratic age. Oscar Wilde was arrested as a gay person, but it was just an extra.

SHIO OKAWA

I see.

GOD THOTH

The part about homosexuality was not his real aim.

SHIO OKAWA

Then, the declining of aristocracy...

GOD THOTH

Yeah, declining a lot.

SHIO OKAWA

Oscar Wilde felt he must let people know?

GOD THOTH

Yeah. Drugs, too much money, gambling, Mahjong, and playing with and abusing or killing lower-class people. They could do whatever they wanted, and they didn't have to take any responsibility.

SHIO OKAWA

Because they didn't need to work to get money.

GOD THOTH

Communism cannot be all good, but it is also true that aristocracy cannot continue as it is. Oscar Wilde was searching for the right way of life for human beings, by trial and error. I think so. One way of human life is, aristocrats think that everything is given to them, but Oscar Wilde was thinking about the importance of the life of giving to other people. He could not do a lot of social activities, so it was not enough for him, but he fought the corruption of aristocracy.

SHIO OKAWA

The spiritual messages from Oscar Wilde make a lot more sense now.

GOD THOTH

So, he failed for his time.

SHIO OKAWA

Yes.

GOD THOTH

Jesus Christ was crucified, which was a failure, and Socrates failed. Oscar Wilde failed in his time, also. He portrayed the world of corruption in the novel, but not only that, he also wanted people to know (that it was wrong) in their real-life experience.

SHIO OKAWA

He experienced it in real life, so he tried to convey that there is something wrong. Is that right?

GOD THOTH

Yes, exactly.

Oscar Wilde did not want to be The God of LGBT

GOD THOTH

At that time, people were addicted to alcohol, gambling, and drugs, and men and women were out of control, sexually. Lower-class women could only sell themselves at that time. So, he wanted to find a way to tell people that it was a problem. I'm sure about that.

SHIO OKAWA

I guess he wanted to insist that every soul is fair and equal in the meaning of its preciousness.

GOD THOTH

Your action can change your mind, and your mind can change your action. I guess he learned the relationship between mind and action. We cannot say that everything he did was for a good reason, but he did not want to be the God of LGBT. I think so.

SHIO OKAWA

So, we should not think about him just from the viewpoint of LGBT.

GOD THOTH

No.

SHIO OKAWA

OK.

GOD THOTH

There were more crimes to be prosecuted, but they were ignored, and instead, a man with affection for boys were sent to jail. It was such kind of society at that time. It's bad. Something was wrong in the laws made by humans and how these were applied. The British way gave birth to Marxism and the revolutions later on. Oscar Wilde could not cover all the social problems.

SHIO OKAWA

OK.

Remember that God is watching you

JIMMU

I have one last question about LGBT. Some Happy Science followers who are LGBT might listen to your spiritual message today and decide to change themselves. Could you please give some words of encouragement for their souls?

GOD THOTH

The subject of men and women is actually the first gateway to a religious character. It's very strict.

SHIO OKAWA

Yes.

GOD THOTH

There is no end to it. "The relationship between men and women. How will you live as a human being? Think about them from the standpoint of a man or a woman." That is one of the starting points for your soul training in this life. Some people are influenced by their surrounding and become similar to them, little by little. I guess so.

My advice is as follows: You might be gay, lesbian or bisexual, but in the Spirit World, people like you created a hell that is a combination of the Hell of Lust and the Hell of Beasts. It already exists. And there, they have no physical bodies, but they are indulging in what they can do with a physical body only. No one can save them.

That is why one religious way is to be innocent or pure. It means you don't take the wrong path. You have many desires because you have physical bodies, and if you make them happen, this world will be a world of stealing, killing, raping, like that. But to make life better for everyone, we must adjust and control the idea that only satisfying all our physical desires means happiness.

So, people make rules, and we must follow them. If you buy a car, you will want to drive at the maximum speed, but the speed limit depends on the road you are driving. It's the same thing. Men rape men, women rape women, and humans have sex with animals; there is such kind of world, in reality. But please remember that God is watching you.

"Do you think God is happy to see such kind of world?" Please think about that.

There is already a hell now. Some spirits said that we will know the results within the next 100 years, but there is already a hell, so the answer is almost clear. There will be more of them, right? So, there is a hell that's different from the hell caused by male-female problems. It means that "sexually out of control" will have a wider meaning.

Regarding this, Jesus said, "If your right eye causes you to sin, tear it out and throw it away." He meant that people are living a wrong way of life because they are attached to the illusions of this world. It means they should control themselves more, and be useful and virtuous for society. If people are not banned from acting on their desires, they cannot protect their family.

You will need a reform in the future

GOD THOTH

LGBT is a difficult problem, but you will need a reform sometime in the future. There are more and more LGBT people in the Western Christian society, especially. Islam is resisting strongly on this part, and I think they are right in some meaning. They are trying to protect their family line.

SHIO OKAWA

Yes.

GOD THOTH

They are right as human beings. If they stop protecting their family line, they will stop respecting their ancestors, and they will lose faith.

SHIO OKAWA

You mean, they will lose gratitude for their parents and others who helped raise them?

GOD THOTH

Yes, that is right.

SHIO OKAWA

The feeling of gratitude will help develop morals, for example, make them think they should control themselves more or repay others who helped them. So, it's not good for this system to be destroyed.

GOD THOTH

No, it's not.

SHIO OKAWA

Morals will be destroyed.

GOD THOTH

If you have no other interest but same-sex love only, you should stay single and live a life of serving God. You can work as a monk or a nun. It's one way of life. But finally, there will be an opposite effect. If you spread LGBT more, there will come a great suppression. I think so.

JIMMU

Thank you very much.

5

Opinion On Islamic Countries

There might be an anti-revolution
To the Iranian Revolution

SHIO OKAWA

Then, next, I want to ask you about the Iran problem.

GOD THOTH

Hmm.

SHIO OKAWA

I think it has to do with Israel, but Iran also has conflicts with Saudi Arabia and the U.S. It's just that, now, Iran is in a crisis; they are about to be attacked. What do you think about this, God Thoth?

GOD THOTH

[*About five seconds of silence.*] In the meaning of civilization, the Islam side is at a disadvantage now, their scientific technology. Advanced nations attack, but they can attack by terrorism or guerilla-like means only. How should I say? Advanced nations understand them (Islam side) like, "They are living like in the primitive age." I think so.

On the other hand, the problem on the Islam side now is... Actually, the problem is more in the oil-producing areas. People there can feed themselves without working, so they are corrupt. They didn't properly create jobs that are in a standard country. People don't have to pay taxes in Saudi Arabia. And, the royal family becomes corrupt. That's Saudi Arabia.

Such kind of society where you don't have to pay taxes because of oil concessions, I mean, a society where you can feed yourself without an ordinary job, is not so good now. But maybe there will come the post-oil age in the near future. At that time, can they survive or not? That's one problem.

SHIO OKAWA

Hmm.

GOD THOTH

But maybe Islam will receive some kind of pressure to reform themselves, I think, because from the Western view, they look totalitarian or something like that, it's true. If they are living for Allah, it's OK. But some Islamic people are using Allah. They think that everything is *inshallah* ("God willing" in Arabic).

SHIO OKAWA

And that's not right, you say?

GOD THOTH

In some meaning, they are fatalists.

SHIO OKAWA

For example, when they are late, they say *inshallah* [*laughs*]. They easily use it.

GOD THOTH

Yeah, yeah. "Allah gave you this homework. Why didn't you do it?" "Allah thinks I don't have to do it." They have such kind of conversation.

SHIO OKAWA

[*Laughs.*] Yes.

GOD THOTH

To put it in a Japanese way, it means we cannot have Jodo Shinshu (True Pure Land Buddhism) manage the country through their idea that, "Bad people will be saved." Islam is like that. They were blessed in some aspect. They were blessed in some age, but it might be time for them to change. So, there is the possibility that there will occur some kind of war. I think so.

SHIO OKAWA

Really?

GOD THOTH

It will be good for them in the meaning of modernization. Khomeini and his followers made a revolution, but an anti-revolution might occur. It's very much possible.

The conflict of Shia and Sunni needs to be resolved sometime. It's not very good for people who believe in the same God to fight or attack or do guerrilla activities to each other. They think that, "Western God is attacking us by means of terrorism," but it's not good. They are wrong. It's not Muhammad's thinking, and it's not Allah's teaching. God of Christianity and Allah of Islam are the same Being. The Quran says so. But now, the opposite is happening.

SHIO OKAWA

Yes.

GOD THOTH

It's a human mistake. There needs some kind of... I think it's not good for a total war to occur, but we should destroy their system and make them reflect. And, we should westernize them a little. I think so. They should speak on common ground (with the Western society).

SHIO OKAWA

Yes, OK.

GOD THOTH

So, I think now is the time to change for China and Islam. The materialistic and atheistic totalitarian nation needs to change, and the totalitarian nations in the name of Allah need to recognize a little more individualism and men and women's rights. They need freedom. In this meaning, Mr. Trump is right, basically.

It's not so bad for Israel-like democracy
To spread in the Middle East

SHIO OKAWA

What do you think about Israel?

GOD THOTH

Israel is a democracy, you know?

SHIO OKAWA

Ah, right, they have elections.

GOD THOTH

If the Israel-like values spread in the Middle East, people there can work and live like the Western people, you know?

SHIO OKAWA

I see.

GOD THOTH

If the God of Israel is right or not is a different problem. In the meaning of spreading democracy, it's not so bad for Israel-like democracy to spread.

New Allah needs to give His teachings

SHIO OKAWA

It's true that Islam has things they should reform, but the West also should fix the part about people becoming arrogant because their democracy went too far, as a result of their values based on "democracy without God."

GOD THOTH

Yes, yes, exactly. Their studies are influenced a lot by atheism and materialism, especially the sciences.

SHIO OKAWA

Right. When we learn Western studies, we can see more materialism and science and pragmatism...

GOD THOTH

Yeah, yeah.

SHIO OKAWA

It's different from what Kant intended, I guess, but the West must fix their thinking that separates God from the rest too much.

GOD THOTH

But Islam will not change, even centuries later, if they stay as it is, I think.

SHIO OKAWA

Right. Hmm.

GOD THOTH

If they use up their oil, they will have nothing.

SHIO OKAWA

They cannot convert, either.

GOD THOTH

No. That's not good.

SHIO OKAWA

Hmm.

GOD THOTH

It's said that Islamic fundamentalists are conducting terrorism, and they are the ones denying change. In reality, what they have been building up is denying change, not God's teachings. So, New Allah needs to give His teachings.

SHIO OKAWA

Yes, right.

GOD THOTH

Relatively speaking, Allah prefers Western democracy. Islam needs to give women the freedom of fashion, freedom to work, freedom to drive, like that. Women are not livestock or property. Islam needs to change things like that. If they have no way to change at this time, then they would need to be perished by a more advanced civilization. I think so.

SHIO OKAWA

You're right. Some parts of Islam have become twisted in later generations, compared to Islam in the age of Muhammad.

GOD THOTH

Islam was a very tolerant religion in the age of Muhammad.

SHIO OKAWA

They were tolerant to women, and other religions, also.

GOD THOTH

Islam was a religion of tolerance and peace. Now, not at all.

SHIO OKAWA

Hmm.

GOD THOTH

They are lacking tolerance a lot, and are the enemies of peace. They must change this.

SHIO OKAWA

Yes.

GOD THOTH

So, Christianity is getting corrupt, but Islam is... All these religious reformations are the mission of El Cantare.

Mr. Trump is trying to start a crusade By working with Israel

SHIO OKAWA

Jesus also said, "Don't make war in the name of Jesus" through his spiritual messages. Both sides have been fighting crusades that are not for justice.

GOD THOTH

Crusades. I think so. Mr. Trump lived at the time of the Crusades in his past life, I think. He is trying to do the Crusades again.

SHIO OKAWA

I see.

GOD THOTH

Now, the U.S. Republican Party is trying to start a crusade again by working with Israel. We cannot help but allow it a little, I guess.

SHIO OKAWA

Hmm.

GOD THOTH

It's just, Islam needs modification to talk and work (with Western people) on common ground.

SHIO OKAWA

You mean, they should be a more open society, right?

GOD THOTH

Yes, yes. That's right. You, Happy Science, also think that Israel is doing too much, and yes, Netanyahu has a problem as a person.

SHIO OKAWA

Prime Minister Netanyahu's personal feeling to intrude is the problem, and...

GOD THOTH

Yeah.

SHIO OKAWA

From a higher point of view, it's not wrong for them (Israel) to aim for a democratic society or a more open Islamic society.

GOD THOTH

Netanyahu can be a dictator as much as he likes, but they will expel him in the end.

SHIO OKAWA

Yes.

GOD THOTH

Because they are a democratic society.

SHIO OKAWA

You're saying they will stop him, right?

GOD THOTH

But the religious leaders of Iran are not expelled.

SHIO OKAWA

You're right.

GOD THOTH

Unless they are attacked by another country. So, it might be different from what you have heard, but you should keep in mind that something like that can happen. We think so. Islam is not totalitarianism, but something similar to that. Of course. They don't change their ways.

SHIO OKAWA

Hmm.

GOD THOTH

That's them.

6

Opinion On North and South Koreas

GOD THOTH

There is one last point, the issue of North and South Koreas. I want to clean up (the issue of) North and South Koreas before the end of the 21st century. I think they will wake up if China goes through a great change because North Korea cannot stay as it is, and South Korea cannot protect themselves by being pro-China.

SHIO OKAWA

That's true. In a way, North and South Koreas can talk aggressively because they have China to rely on.

GOD THOTH

Yeah. North Korea can survive because over 90 percent of their trade is with China. And

South Korea thinks they can survive if they just have connections with China, even if they lose connections with Japan or America. I'm planning on resolving this in the next several years.

SHIO OKAWA
OK. Then...

GOD THOTH
Is that enough?

SHIO OKAWA & JIMMU
Yes.

GOD THOTH
OK. I'm sorry that I spoke on the content of Master's lecture tomorrow.

SHIO OKAWA
No, it's OK. Tomorrow's lecture is short, just 40 minutes, so Master Ryuho Okawa cannot talk

about everything. That's why we asked you what you think, before the lecture, to cover what Master cannot talk about.

GOD THOTH
OK. This is what the God governing North America is thinking about now.

SHIO OKAWA
OK. We're sorry for the trouble.

GOD THOTH
OK.

JIMMU
Thank you.

ABOUT THE AUTHOR

Founder and CEO of Happy Science Group.

Ryuho Okawa was born on July 7th 1956, in Tokushima, Japan. After graduating from the University of Tokyo with a law degree, he joined a Tokyo-based trading house. While working at its New York headquarters, he studied international finance at the Graduate Center of the City University of New York. In 1981, he attained Great Enlightenment and became aware that he is El Cantare with a mission to bring salvation to all humankind.

In 1986, he established Happy Science. It now has members in over 165 countries across the world, with more than 700 branches and temples as well as 10,000 missionary houses around the world.

He has given over 3,400 lectures (of which more than 150 are in English) and published over 3,000 books (of which more than 600 are Spiritual Interview Series), and many are translated into 40 languages. Along with *The Laws of the Sun* and *The Laws Of Messiah*, many of the books have become best sellers or million sellers. To date, Happy Science has produced 25 movies. The original story and original concept were given by the Executive Producer Ryuho Okawa. He has also composed music and written lyrics of over 450 pieces.

Moreover, he is the Founder of Happy Science University and Happy Science Academy (Junior and Senior High School), Founder and President of the Happiness Realization Party, Founder and Honorary Headmaster of Happy Science Institute of Government and Management, Founder of IRH Press Co., Ltd., and the Chairperson of NEW STAR PRODUCTION Co., Ltd. and ARI Production Co., Ltd.

WHAT IS EL CANTARE?

El Cantare means "the Light of the Earth," and is the Supreme God of the Earth who has been guiding humankind since the beginning of Genesis. He is whom Jesus called Father and Muhammad called Allah, and is *Ame-no-Mioya-Gami*, Japanese Father God. Different parts of El Cantare's core consciousness have descended to Earth in the past, once as Alpha and another as Elohim. His branch spirits, such as Shakyamuni Buddha and Hermes, have descended to Earth many times and helped to flourish many civilizations. To unite various religions and to integrate various fields of study in order to build a new civilization on Earth, a part of the core consciousness has descended to Earth as Master Ryuho Okawa.

Alpha is a part of the core consciousness of El Cantare who descended to Earth around 330 million years ago. Alpha preached Earth's Truths to harmonize and unify Earth-born humans and space people who came from other planets.

Elohim is a part of El Cantare's core consciousness who descended to Earth around 150 million years ago. He gave wisdom, mainly on the differences of light and darkness, good and evil.

Ame-no-Mioya-Gami (Japanese Father God) is the Creator God and the Father God who appears in the ancient literature, *Hotsuma Tsutae*. It is believed that He descended on the foothills of Mt. Fuji about 30,000 years ago and built the Fuji dynasty, which is the root of the Japanese civilization. With justice as the central pillar, Ame-no-Mioya-Gami's teachings spread to ancient civilizations of other countries in the world.

Shakyamuni Buddha was born as a prince into the Shakya Clan in India around 2,600 years ago. When he was 29 years old, he renounced the world and sought enlightenment. He later attained Great Enlightenment and founded Buddhism.

Hermes is one of the 12 Olympian gods in Greek mythology, but the spiritual Truth is that he taught the teachings of love and progress around 4,300 years ago that became the origin of the current Western civilization. He is a hero that truly existed.

Ophealis was born in Greece around 6,500 years ago and was the leader who took an expedition to as far as Egypt. He is the God of miracles, prosperity, and arts, and is known as Osiris in the Egyptian mythology.

Rient Arl Croud was born as a king of the ancient Incan Empire around 7,000 years ago and taught about the mysteries of the mind. In the heavenly world, he is responsible for the interactions that take place between various planets.

Thoth was an almighty leader who built the golden age of the Atlantic civilization around 12,000 years ago. In the Egyptian mythology, he is known as god Thoth.

Ra Mu was a leader who built the golden age of the civilization of Mu around 17,000 years ago. As a religious leader and a politician, he ruled by uniting religion and politics.

WHAT IS A SPIRITUAL MESSAGE?

We are all spiritual beings living on this earth. The following is the mechanism behind Master Ryuho Okawa's spiritual messages.

1 You are a spirit

People are born into this world to gain wisdom through various experiences and return to the other world when their lives end. We are all spirits and repeat this cycle in order to refine our souls.

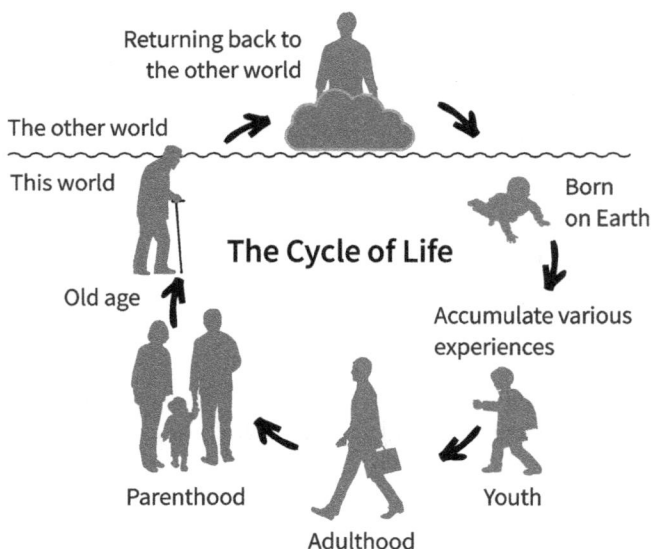

Returning back to
the other world

The other world

This world

Born
on Earth

The Cycle of Life

Old age

Accumulate various
experiences

Parenthood

Youth

Adulthood

2 You have a guardian spirit

Guardian spirits are those who protect the people who are living on this earth. Each of us has a guardian spirit that watches over us and guides us from the other world. They were us in our past life, and are identical in how we think.

3 How spiritual messages work

Master Ryuho Okawa, through his enlightenment, is capable of summoning any spirit from anywhere in the world, including the spirit world.

Master Okawa's way of receiving spiritual messages is fundamentally different from that of other psychic mediums who undergo trances and are thereby completely taken over by the spirits they are channeling.

Master Okawa's attainment of a high level of enlightenment enables him to retain full control of his consciousness and body throughout the duration of the spiritual message. To allow the spirits to express their own thoughts and personalities freely, however, Master Okawa usually softens the dominancy of his consciousness. This way, he is able to keep his own philosophies out of the way and ensure that the spiritual messages are pure expressions of the spirits he is channeling.

Since guardian spirits think at the same subconscious level as the person living on earth, Master Okawa can summon the spirit and find out what the person on earth is actually thinking. If the person has already returned to the other world, the spirit can give messages to the people living on earth through Master Okawa.

Since 2009, many spiritual messages have been openly recorded by Master Okawa and published. Spiritual messages from the guardian spirits of people living today such as Donald Trump, former Japanese Prime Minister Shinzo Abe and Chinese President Xi Jinping, as well as spiritual messages sent from the spirit world by Jesus Christ, Muhammad, Thomas Edison, Mother Teresa, Steve Jobs and Nelson Mandela are just a tiny pack of spiritual messages that were published so far.

Domestically, in Japan, these spiritual messages are being read by a wide range of politicians and mass media, and the high-level contents of these books are delivering an impact even more on politics, news and public opinion. In recent years, there have been spiritual messages recorded in English, and

English translations are being done on the spiritual messages given in Japanese. These have been published overseas, one after another, and have started to shake the world.

1. The guardian spirit / spirit in the other world...

2. Goes inside Master Okawa in this world

3. Master Okawa speaks the words of the guardian spirit / spirit

For more about spiritual messages and a complete list of books in the Spiritual Interview Series, visit okawabooks.com

ABOUT HAPPY SCIENCE

Happy Science is a global movement that empowers individuals to find purpose and spiritual happiness and to share that happiness with their families, societies, and the world. With more than 12 million members around the world, Happy Science aims to increase awareness of spiritual truths and expand our capacity for love, compassion, and joy so that together we can create the kind of world we all wish to live in.

Activities at Happy Science are based on the Principle of Happiness (Love, Wisdom, Self-Reflection, and Progress). This principle embraces worldwide philosophies and beliefs, transcending boundaries of culture and religions.

Love teaches us to give ourselves freely without expecting anything in return; it encompasses giving, nurturing, and forgiving.

Wisdom leads us to the insights of spiritual truths, and opens us to the true meaning of life and the will of God (the universe, the highest power, Buddha).

Self-Reflection brings a mindful, nonjudgmental lens to our thoughts and actions to help us find our truest selves—the essence of our souls—and deepen our connection to the highest power. It helps us attain a clean and peaceful mind and leads us to the right life path.

Progress emphasizes the positive, dynamic aspects of our spiritual growth—actions we can take to manifest and spread happiness around the world. It's a path that not only expands our soul growth, but also furthers the collective potential of the world we live in.

PROGRAMS AND EVENTS

The doors of Happy Science are open to all. We offer a variety of programs and events, including self-exploration and self-growth programs, spiritual seminars, meditation and contemplation sessions, study groups, and book events.

Our programs are designed to:
* Deepen your understanding of your purpose and meaning in life
* Improve your relationships and increase your capacity to love unconditionally
* Attain peace of mind, decrease anxiety and stress, and feel positive
* Gain deeper insights and a broader perspective on the world
* Learn how to overcome life's challenges
  ... and much more.

For more information, visit happy-science.org.

OUR ACTIVITIES

Happy Science does other various activities to provide support for those in need.

◆ **You Are An Angel! General Incorporated Association**

Happy Science has a volunteer network in Japan that encourages and supports children with disabilities as well as their parents and guardians.

◆ **Never Mind School for Truancy**

At 'Never Mind,' we support students who find it very challenging to attend schools in Japan. We also nurture their self-help spirit and power to rebound against obstacles in life based on Master Okawa's teachings and faith.

◆ **"Prevention Against Suicide" Campaign since 2003**

A nationwide campaign to reduce suicides; over 20,000 people commit suicide every year in Japan. "The Suicide Prevention Website-Words of Truth for You-" presents spiritual prescriptions for worries such as depression, lost love, extramarital affairs, bullying and work-related problems, thereby saving many lives.

◆ **Support for Anti-bullying Campaigns**

Happy Science provides support for a group of parents and guardians, Network to Protect Children from Bullying, a general incorporated foundation launched in Japan to end bullying, including those that can even be called a criminal offense. So far, the network received more than 5,000 cases and resolved 90% of them.

◆ **The Golden Age Scholarship**

This scholarship is granted to students who can contribute greatly and bring a hopeful future to the world.

◆ **Success No.1**
Buddha's Truth Afterschool Academy

Happy Science has over 180 classrooms throughout Japan and in several cities around the world that focus on afterschool education for children. The education focuses on faith and morals in addition to supporting children's school studies.

◆ **Angel Plan V**

For children under the age of kindergarten, Happy Science holds classes for nurturing healthy, positive, and creative boys and girls.

◆ **Future Stars Training Department**

The Future Stars Training Department was founded within the Happy Science Media Division with the goal of nurturing talented individuals to become successful in the performing arts and entertainment industry.

◆ **NEW STAR PRODUCTION Co., Ltd.**
ARI Production Co., Ltd.

We have companies to nurture actors and actresses, artists, and vocalists. They are also involved in film production.

CONTACT INFORMATION

Happy Science is a worldwide organization with branches and temples around the globe. For a comprehensive list, visit the worldwide directory at *happy-science.org*. The following are some of the many Happy Science locations:

UNITED STATES AND CANADA

New York
79 Franklin St., New York, NY 10013, USA
Phone: 1-212-343-7972
Fax: 1-212-343-7973
Email: ny@happy-science.org
Website: happyscience-usa.org

New Jersey
66 Hudson St., #2R, Hoboken, NJ 07030, USA
Phone: 1-201-313-0127
Email: nj@happy-science.org
Website: happyscience-usa.org

Chicago
2300 Barrington Rd., Suite #400,
Hoffman Estates, IL 60169, USA
Phone: 1-630-937-3077
Email: chicago@happy-science.org
Website: happyscience-usa.org

Florida
5208 8th St., Zephyrhills, FL 33542, USA
Phone: 1-813-715-0000
Fax: 1-813-715-0010
Email: florida@happy-science.org
Website: happyscience-usa.org

Atlanta
1874 Piedmont Ave., NE Suite 360-C
Atlanta, GA 30324, USA
Phone: 1-404-892-7770
Email: atlanta@happy-science.org
Website: happyscience-usa.org

San Francisco
525 Clinton St.
Redwood City, CA 94062, USA
Phone & Fax: 1-650-363-2777
Email: sf@happy-science.org
Website: happyscience-usa.org

Los Angeles
1590 E. Del Mar Blvd., Pasadena, CA
91106, USA
Phone: 1-626-395-7775
Fax: 1-626-395-7776
Email: la@happy-science.org
Website: happyscience-usa.org

Orange County
16541 Gothard St. Suite 104
Huntington Beach, CA 92647
Phone: 1-714-659-1501
Email: oc@happy-science.org
Website: happyscience-usa.org

San Diego
7841 Balboa Ave. Suite #202
San Diego, CA 92111, USA
Phone: 1-626-395-7775
Fax: 1-626-395-7776
E-mail: sandiego@happy-science.org
Website: happyscience-usa.org

Hawaii
Phone: 1-808-591-9772
Fax: 1-808-591-9776
Email: hi@happy-science.org
Website: happyscience-usa.org

Kauai
3343 Kanakolu Street, Suite 5
Lihue, HI 96766, USA
Phone: 1-808-822-7007
Fax: 1-808-822-6007
Email: kauai-hi@happy-science.org
Website: happyscience-usa.org

Toronto
845 The Queensway
Etobicoke, ON M8Z 1N6, Canada
Phone: 1-416-901-3747
Email: toronto@happy-science.org
Website: happy-science.ca

Vancouver
#201-2607 East 49th Avenue,
Vancouver, BC, V5S 1J9, Canada
Phone: 1-604-437-7735
Fax: 1-604-437-7764
Email: vancouver@happy-science.org
Website: happy-science.ca

INTERNATIONAL

Tokyo
1-6-7 Togoshi, Shinagawa,
Tokyo, 142-0041, Japan
Phone: 81-3-6384-5770
Fax: 81-3-6384-5776
Email: tokyo@happy-science.org
Website: happy-science.org

Seoul
74, Sadang-ro 27-gil,
Dongjak-gu, Seoul, Korea
Phone: 82-2-3478-8777
Fax: 82-2-3478-9777
Email: korea@happy-science.org
Website: happyscience-korea.org

London
3 Margaret St.
London, W1W 8RE United Kingdom
Phone: 44-20-7323-9255
Fax: 44-20-7323-9344
Email: eu@happy-science.org
Website: www.happyscience-uk.org

Taipei
No. 89, Lane 155, Dunhua N. Road,
Songshan District, Taipei City 105, Taiwan
Phone: 886-2-2719-9377
Fax: 886-2-2719-5570
Email: taiwan@happy-science.org
Website: happyscience-tw.org

Sydney
516 Pacific Highway, Lane Cove North,
2066 NSW, Australia
Phone: 61-2-9411-2877
Fax: 61-2-9411-2822
Email: sydney@happy-science.org

Kuala Lumpur
No 22A, Block 2, Jalil Link Jalan Jalil
Jaya 2, Bukit Jalil 57000,
Kuala Lumpur, Malaysia
Phone: 60-3-8998-7877
Fax: 60-3-8998-7977
Email: malaysia@happy-science.org
Website: happyscience.org.my

Sao Paulo
Rua. Domingos de Morais 1154,
Vila Mariana, Sao Paulo SP
CEP 04010-100, Brazil
Phone: 55-11-5088-3800
Email: sp@happy-science.org
Website: happyscience.com.br

Kathmandu
Kathmandu Metropolitan City,
Ward No. 15, Ring Road, Kimdol,
Sitapaila Kathmandu, Nepal
Phone: 977-1-427-2931
Email: nepal@happy-science.org

Jundiai
Rua Congo, 447, Jd. Bonfiglioli
Jundiai-CEP, 13207-340, Brazil
Phone: 55-11-4587-5952
Email: jundiai@happy-science.org

Kampala
Plot 877 Rubaga Road, Kampala
P.O. Box 34130 Kampala, UGANDA
Phone: 256-79-4682-121
Email: uganda@happy-science.org

The Happiness Realization Party (HRP) was founded in May 2009 by Master Ryuho Okawa as part of the Happy Science Group. HRP strives to improve the Japanese society, based on three basic political principles of "freedom, democracy, and faith," and let Japan promote individual and public happiness from Asia to the world as a leader nation.

1) Diplomacy and Security: Protecting Freedom, Democracy, and Faith of Japan and the World from China's Totalitarianism

Japan's current defense system is insufficient against China's expanding hegemony and the threat of North Korea's nuclear missiles. Japan, as the leader of Asia, must strengthen its defense power and promote strategic diplomacy together with the nations which share the values of freedom, democracy, and faith. Further, HRP aims to realize world peace under the leadership of Japan, the nation with the spirit of religious tolerance.

2) Economy: Early economic recovery through utilizing the "wisdom of the private sector"

Economy has been damaged severely by the novel coronavirus originated in China. Many companies have been forced into bankruptcy or out of business. What is needed for economic recovery now is not subsidies and regulations by the government, but policies which can utilize the "wisdom of the private sector."

For more information, visit en.hr-party.jp

ABOUT HS PRESS

HS Press is an imprint of IRH Press Co., Ltd. IRH Press Co., Ltd., based in Tokyo, was founded in 1987 as a publishing division of Happy Science. IRH Press publishes religious and spiritual books, journals, magazines and also operates broadcast and film production enterprises. For more information, visit *okawabooks.com*.

Follow us on:

f Facebook: Okawa Books ⓘ Instagram: OkawaBooks

▶ Youtube: Okawa Books 🐦 Twitter: Okawa Books

𝓟 Pinterest: Okawa Books g Goodreads: Ryuho Okawa

——— **NEWSLETTER** ———

To receive book related news, promotions and events, please subscribe to our newsletter below.

🔗 eepurl.com/bsMeJj

 ——— **AUDIO / VISUAL MEDIA** ———

YOUTUBE   **PODCAST**

Introduction of Ryuho Okawa's titles; topics ranging from self-help, current affairs, spirituality, religion, and the universe.

BOOKS BY RYUHO OKAWA

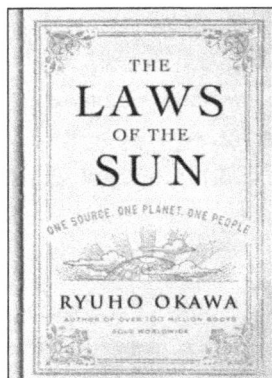

THE LAWS OF THE SUN
ONE SOURCE, ONE PLANET, ONE PEOPLE

Paperback • 288 pages • $15.95
ISBN: 978-1-942125-43-3

IMAGINE IF YOU COULD ASK GOD why He created this world and what spiritual laws He used to shape us—and everything around us. If we could understand His designs and intentions, we could discover what our goals in life should be and whether our actions move us closer to those goals or farther away.

At a young age, a spiritual calling prompted Ryuho Okawa to outline what he innately understood to be universal truths for all humankind. In *The Laws of the Sun*, Okawa outlines these laws of the universe and provides a road map for living one's life with greater purpose and meaning.

In this powerful book, Ryuho Okawa reveals the transcendent nature of consciousness and the secrets of our multidimensional universe and our place in it. By understanding the different stages of love and following the Buddhist Eightfold Path, he believes we can speed up our eternal process of development. *The Laws of the Sun* shows the way to realize true happiness—a happiness that continues from this world through the other.

For a complete list of books, visit **okawabooks.com**

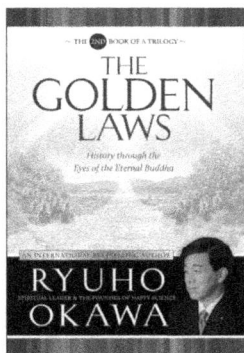

THE GOLDEN LAWS

HISTORY THROUGH THE EYES OF THE ETERNAL BUDDHA

Paperback • 201 pages • $14.95
ISBN: 978-1-941779-81-1

Throughout history, Great Guiding Spirits of Light have been present on Earth in both the East and the West at crucial points in human history to further our spiritual development. *The Golden Laws* reveals how Divine Plan has been unfolding on Earth, and outlines 5,000 years of the secret history of humankind. Once we understand the true course of history, through past, present and into the future, we cannot help but become aware of the significance of our spiritual mission in the present age.

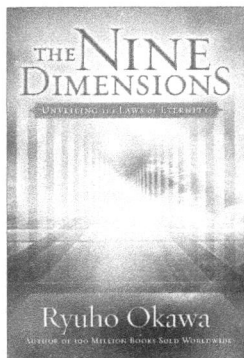

THE NINE DIMENSIONS

UNVEILING THE LAWS OF ETERNITY

Paperback • 168 pages • $15.95
ISBN: 978-0-982698-56-3

This book is a window into the mind of our loving God, who designed this world and the vast, wondrous world of our afterlife as a school with many levels through which our souls learn and grow. When the religions and cultures of the world discover the truth of their common spiritual origin, they will be inspired to accept their differences, come together under faith in God, and build an era of harmony and peaceful progress on Earth.

---

*For a complete list of books, visit **okawabooks.com***

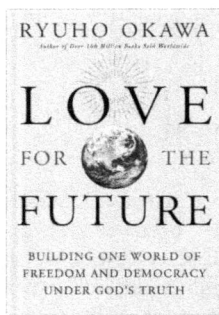

LOVE FOR THE FUTURE

BUILDING ONE WORLD OF FREEDOM AND DEMOCRACY UNDER GOD'S TRUTH

Paperback • 312 pages • $15.95
ISBN: 978-1-942125-60-0

This is a compilation of select international lectures given by Ryuho Okawa during his (ongoing) global missionary tours. It espouses that freedom and democracy are vital principles to foster peace and shared prosperity, if adopted universally.

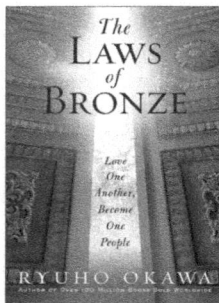

THE LAWS OF BRONZE

LOVE ONE ANOTHER, BECOME ONE PEOPLE

Paperback • 224 pages • $15.95
ISBN: 978-1-942125-50-1

This is the 25th volume of the Laws Series by Ryuho Okawa. This miraculous and inspiring book will show the keys to living a spiritual life of truth regardless of their age, gender, or race.

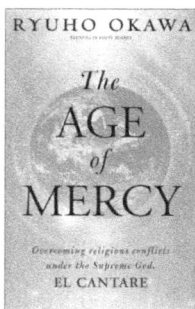

THE AGE OF MERCY

OVERCOMING RELIGIOUS CONFLICTS UNDER THE SUPREME GOD, EL CANTARE

Hardcover • 110 pages • $22.95
ISBN: 978-1-943869-51-0

Why are there conflicts in the world? How can people understand each other better? This book is a message from the Supreme God who has been guiding humankind from the beginning of creation.

For a complete list of books, visit **okawabooks.com**

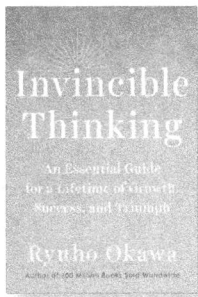

INVINCIBLE THINKING
AN ESSENTIAL GUIDE FOR A LIFETIME OF GROWTH, SUCCESS, AND TRIUMPH

Hardcover • 208 pages • $16.95
ISBN: 978-1-942125-25-9

In this book, Ryuho Okawa lays out the principles of invincible thinking that will allow us to achieve long-lasting triumph. This powerful and unique philosophy is not only about becoming successful or achieving our goal in life, but also about building the foundation of life that becomes the basis of our life-long, lasting success and happiness.

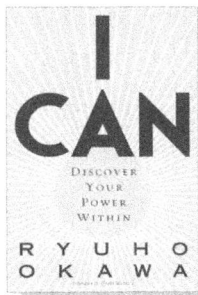

I CAN
DISCOVER YOUR POWER WITHIN

Paperback • 103 pages • $14.95
ISBN: 978-1-937673-25-3

There are countless books on self-development, but none as deep and religious as *I Can -Discover Your Power Within-* by Ryuho Okawa. In this enlightening masterpiece by Okawa, the Master and CEO of Happy Science, you can gain stronger confidence in yourself, overcome adversities and anxieties, and make your dreams come true by learning the spirit of self-help and by knowing the secret to your creative power within.

INTO THE STORM OF INTERNATIONAL POLITICS
THE NEW STANDARDS OF THE WORLD ORDER

Paperback • 154 pages • $14.95
ISBN:978-1-941779-27-9

The world is now seeking a new idea or a new philosophy that will show the countries with such values the direction they should head in. In this book, Okawa presents new standards of the world order while giving his own analysis on world affairs concerning the U.S., China, Islamic State and others.

---

*For a complete list of books, visit **okawabooks.com***

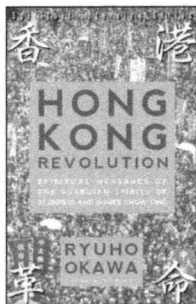

Hong Kong Revolution

Spiritual Messages of the Guardian Spirits of Xi Jinping and Agnes Chow Ting

Paperback • 282 pages • $13.95
ISBN: 978-1-943869-55-8

The Hong Kong protests that are gathering the attention of the world. What is Xi Jinping plotting? How far is Agnes Chow, the 'Goddess of Democracy,' willing to go? Their guardian spirits sreveal issues of conflict in this exciting new book!

Spiritual Interview with the Guardian Spirit of Joshua Wong

His resolve to protect the freedom of Hong Kong

Paperback • 82 pages • $9.95
ISBN:978-1-943869-54-1

To those around the world who believe in God and pray for God's justice to be served, we hereby bring you the words of the guardian spirit of Joshua Wong Let there be glory in his courage and the freedom of Hong Kong.

Spiritual Messages from Oscar Wilde

Love, Beauty, and LGBT

Paperback • 80 pages • $9.95
ISBN:978-1-943869-50-3

Why did Oscar Wilde write the Happy Prince?
The Astonishing Truth:
- His spiritual connection to Jesus Christ
- The deeper meaning behind his homosexuality
- Advice for the LGBT people to become happy

For a complete list of books, visit **okawabooks.com**

THE LAWS OF GREAT ENLIGHTENMENT
Always Walk with Buddha

THE LAWS OF INVINCIBLE LEADERSHIP
An Empowering Guide for Continuous and
Lasting Success in Business and in Life

THE STARTING POINT OF HAPPINESS
An Inspiring Guide to Positive Living with Faith, Love, and Courage

HEALING FROM WITHIN
Life-Changing Keys to Calm, Spiritual, and Healthy Living

THE UNHAPPINESS SYNDROME
28 Habits of Unhappy People (and How to Change Them)

THE LAWS OF SUCCESS
A Spiritual Guide to Turning Your Hopes Into Reality

THINK BIG!
Be Positive and Be Brave to Achieve Your Dreams

RYUHO OKAWA
A POLITICAL REVOLUTIONARY
The Originator of Abenomics and
Father of the Happiness Realization Party

THE MOMENT OF TRUTH
Become a Living Angel Today

CHANGE YOUR LIFE, CHANGE THE WORLD
A Spiritual Guide to Living Now

For a complete list of books, visit **okawabooks.com**

MUSIC BY RYUHO OKAWA

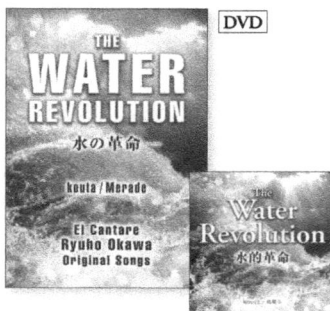

With Savior *English version*

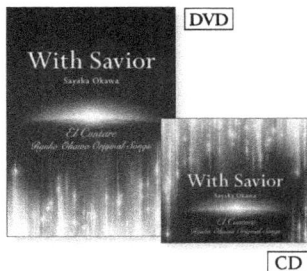
DVD

With Savior
Sayaka Okawa

With Savior
Sayaka Okawa

CD

This is the message of hope to the modern people who are living in the midst of the Coronavirus pandemic, natural disasters, economic depression, and other various crises.

Search on YouTube

with savior 🔍 for a short ad!

The Thunder
a composition for repelling the Coronavirus

We have been granted this music from our Lord. It will repel away the novel Coronavirus originated in China. Experience this magnificent powerful music.

Search on YouTube

the thunder composition 🔍

for a short ad!

THE THUNDER
a composition for repelling the Coronavirus
CD

The Exorcism
prayer music for repelling Lost Spirits

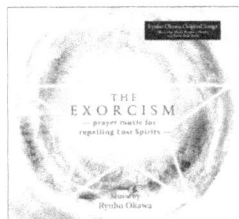
THE EXORCISM
prayer music for repelling Lost Spirits
CD

Feel the divine vibrations of this Japanese and Western exorcising symphony to banish all evil possessions you suffer from and to purify your space!

Search on YouTube

the exorcism repelling 🔍

for a short ad!

Listen now today!
Download from
🎧 **Spotify iTunes Amazon**

DVD, CD available at amazon.com, and Happy Science locations worldwide